P9-BXW-069

PENGUIN BOOKS

PRESIDENTIAL WIT AND WISDOM

Jess Brallier is a book publisher and author. Sally Chabert graduated from college with a degree in political science, held various
positions in the book publishing industry, and is now a ghostwriter.
Coauthors of *Celebrate America*, they are married and live in
Reading, Massachusetts.

Brallier's books include the best-selling *Lawyers and Other Rep-
tiles*, *Medical Wit and Wisdom*, and *The Hot Dog Cookbook*. He
is coauthor of *Write Your Own Living Will*, two editions of *The
Pessimist's Journal of Very, Very Bad Days*, and *The Really, Really
Classy Donald Trump Quiz Book*.

PRESIDENTIAL
WIT AND WISDOM

★ ★ ★

MAXIMS, MOTTOES, SOUND BITES, SPEECHES, AND ASIDES

Memorable Quotes from America's Presidents

JESS BRALLIER AND
SALLY CHABERT

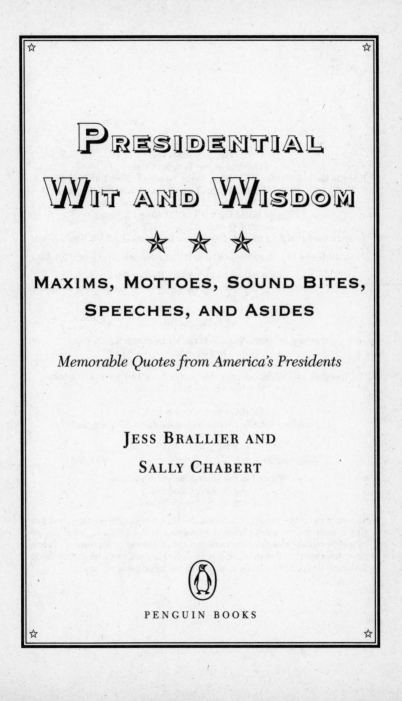

PENGUIN BOOKS

PENGUIN BOOKS
Published by the Penguin Group
Penguin Books USA Inc., 375 Hudson Street, New York, New York 10014, U.S.A.
Penguin Books Ltd, 27 Wrights Lane, London W8 5TZ, England
Penguin Books Australia Ltd, Ringwood, Victoria, Australia
Penguin Books Canada Ltd, 10 Alcorn Avenue,
Toronto, Ontario, Canada M4V 3B2
Penguin Books (N.Z.) Ltd, 182–190 Wairau Road, Auckland 10, New Zealand

Penguin Books Ltd, Registered Offices: Harmondsworth, Middlesex, England

First published in Penguin Books 1996

1 3 5 7 9 10 8 6 4 2

Copyright © Jess Brallier and Sally Chabert, 1996
All rights reserved

LIBRARY OF CONGRESS CATALOGING IN PUBLICATION DATA
Brallier, Jess.
Presidential wit and wisdom : maxims, mottoes, sound bites,
speeches, and asides—memorable quotes from America's presidents /
Jess Brallier and Sally Chabert.
p. cm.
ISBN 0 14 02.3904 9 (pbk.)
1. Presidents—United States—Quotations. I. Chabert, Sally.
II. Title.
E176.1.B84 1996
973'.099—dc20 95–23184

Printed in the United States of America
Set in New Caledonia
Designed by Jessica Shatan

Except in the United States of America, this book is sold subject to the condition
that it shall not, by way of trade or otherwise, be lent, re-sold, hired out, or
otherwise circulated without the publisher's prior consent in any form of binding
or cover other than that in which it is published and without a similar condition
including this condition being imposed on the subsequent purchaser.

To Sally
—JMB

To Jess
—SCC

The White House is a bully pulpit.

—PRESIDENT THEODORE ROOSEVELT

Making up presidential quotes is not lying. When you're a press secretary, you develop a bond of understanding with the President so that you think like the President. I knew those quotes were the way he felt.

—LARRY SPEAKES
press secretary
to President Ronald Reagan

☆ CONTENTS ☆

☆ INTRODUCTION ☆

A good quotation is a wonderful thing. It may inspire, amuse, or enlighten. Better yet, it may do all three.

Researching and compiling this collection was laborious, fascinating, and a very special and privileged opportunity. Quotes are so special that the book where John Bartlett first gathered his collection in 1855 is now in its sixteenth edition and still selling by the thousands every month. There are another five hundred collections of quotes in print, books compiled for any imaginable group: women, lawyers, middle managers, cooks, gardeners, lovers. There's a quote or two for everybody; and for every quote, an admirer or two. A love of quotations puts one in very good company:

I love quotations, because it is a joy to find thoughts one might have beautifully expressed with much authority by someone recognizably wiser than oneself.
—Marlene Dietrich

It is a good thing for an uneducated man to read books of quotations.
—Winston Churchill

Nothing gives an author so much pleasure as to find his works respectfully quoted.
—Benjamin Franklin

A great man quotes bravely.
—Ralph Waldo Emerson

What America's presidents write and say makes for an especially fertile and unique source of quotations. After all, these men belong to a very exclusive club—its membership numbers only forty-one. They wield great power and influence yet do so very publicly. They live their lives at the extremes of the human condition, and we expect them to report—at least, comment upon—those extremes. We expect that what they say will sometimes inspire or motivate us and at other moments, comfort and reassure. As a nation, we look upon these individuals and expect, even demand, to know what they think and feel. This is the very stuff of great quotations. It is only logical that a collection of presidential quotations should be an especially rich one.

Several presidents were among those brilliant few who founded the nation and in the process authored the Declaration of Independence and created the United States Constitution. All presidents faced the agony of sending loved ones to die, on battlefields from Virginia to Iraq. One president, in presiding over a country torn apart by civil war, provided the greatest presidential quotation of all: the "Gettysburg Address." One president chose to develop the atomic bomb, another decided to use it. All the presidents, like each of us, suffered the tragic loss of family and friends. Each president, in some way, lessened the quality of life for certain people and enriched the lives of others. Some presidents lived busy lives, others quite simple ones. Every president suffered from criticism, loss, and uncertainty. And none escaped the scrutiny of the press or biographer.

It is our intention that in these pages you will find the promised wit and wisdom, but that you will also hear the American language develop (compare Jefferson with Bush); witness the incursion and influence of the electronic media (from Franklin Roosevelt to Bill Clinton); and recognize drastic and enduring shifts in the very purpose of government (contrast Madison and Monroe with FDR and LBJ).

Quotes cast any subject in a clear light, and we hope that these presidential quotations will illuminate not only the man who spoke them and the issues he faced, but also the complex history of a nation and its highest office.

> JESS BRALLIER
> SALLY CHABERT
> The Captain James Bancroft* House
> Massachusetts
> 1995

---

* "the faithful Bancroft"
—George Washington

PRESIDENTIAL
WIT AND WISDOM

☆ GEORGE WASHINGTON ☆

1st President

Birth: February 22, 1732   Death: December 14, 1799
Term: April 30, 1789–March 3, 1797

THE WASHINGTON PRESIDENCY

- *The country's first presidency*
- *First United States census authorized (1790)*
- *First session of United States Supreme Court (1790)*
- *Vermont (1791), Kentucky (1792), and Tennessee (1796) admitted as states*
- *District of Columbia established (1791)*
- *Bill of Rights (first ten amendments to the Constitution) ratified (1791)*
- *Cornerstones of both White House (1792) and Capitol (1793) laid*

The "Father of our Country" was probably not a father at all. Although George Washington adopted his wife's two children from a previous marriage, he had no natural offspring.

In 1782, with the British defeated and the independence of the American Colonies assured, it was proposed that Washington become the first king of the new nation. Although he declined, Washington did believe that as the chief officer of a new nation, he should present a dignified appearance. Ironically, it was the king of England —his only model at that time—after whom Washington fashioned his behavior. He insisted on formal dress and, whenever traveling, he went about in a beautiful carriage pulled by handsome horses.

Born and raised on the family farm in Virginia which his great-grandfather, a native of England, had settled, Washington worked as a surveyor for several years in his late teens. Beginning in 1752, he served with the Virginia militia during the French and Indian War until the end of 1758 when he was elected to the Virginia House of Burgesses. During this tenure of his military career, while serving as aide-de-camp to British General Edward Braddock, Washington suffered a humiliating defeat at Fort Necessity in western Pennsylvania.

Meanwhile, having similar poor luck on the love front, the girl-shy lad was moved to write classic verse such as . . .

Ah! woe's me, that should love and conceal,
I wish, but never dare reveal,
Even though severely Love's Pains I feel.

Washington's love interests included Mary Phillpse (although some wonder if he was as taken with her personality as he was with her wealthy father's 51,000 acres) and Sally Fairfax, who was married to Washington's friend and neighbor, George William Fairfax. Later, during the American Revolution, both Mary and Sally and their husbands were staunch Tories. Eventually, at the age of twenty-six, Washington married Martha Dandridge Custis, a widow with two children and the wealthiest marriageable woman in Virginia.

After serving as a delegate to the Continental Congress (1774–75), Washington was appointed commander in chief of the Continental Army (1775–83). Most military experts believe that he was a good general but not a great one. His army lost more battles than it won. But the core of his army was never destroyed or captured. Washington insisted that as long as the Americans could keep an army in the field, the British could not win. And on that score, he was proved right, against great odds.

Washington was the obvious choice for the first president of the United States. Not even one of the sixty-nine electors voted against him. He carried all ten states (North Carolina and Rhode Island had not yet ratified the Constitution, and New York failed to submit its electors in time). Thus Washington is the only president to have been elected by a unanimous electoral vote.

On April 30, 1789, Washington stood on the balcony of Federal Hall in New York City, and slowly, solemnly, took the oath that made him president of the United States.

I walk on untrodden ground. There is scarcely any part of my conduct that may not hereafter be drawn into precedent.

Of his presidency, Washington said, "Many things which appear of little importance in themselves and at the beginning may have great and durable consequences from their having been established at the commencement of a new general government." Washington therefore conducted his administration with caution, acting only when it seemed necessary to flesh out the bare framework of government so sparingly described in the Constitution. After serving two terms, he returned to his beloved Mount Vernon in 1797. In 1799, he was caught in a snowstorm while riding about the estate. Two days later he spoke, weakly, to his aide:

I am just going. Have me decently buried and do not let my body be into a vault in less than two days after I am dead. Do you understand me? ("Yes," replied the aide.) 'Tis well.

Those were his last words.

★　★　★

If I should conceive myself in a manner constrained to accept, I call Heaven to witness, that this very act [acceptance of the presidency] would be the greatest sacrifice of my personal feelings and wishes that ever I have been called upon to make.

I walk on untrodden ground. There is scarcely any part of my conduct which may not hereafter be drawn into precedent.
(on the presidency)

My movements to the chair of Government will be accompanied by feelings not unlike those of a culprit who is going to the place of his execution.
(on the presidency)

I am embarked on a wide ocean, boundless in its prospect and in which, perhaps, no safe harbor is to be found.
(on his appointment as commander in chief)

There is nothing so likely to produce peace as to be well prepared to meet an enemy.

The preservation of the sacred fire of liberty and the destiny of the republican model of government are justly considered, perhaps as *deeply*, and *finally*, staked on the experiment entrusted to the hands of the American people.

The basis of our political systems is the right of the people to make and to alter their constitutions of government. But the constitution, which at any time exists, until changed by an explicit and authentic act of the whole people, is sacredly obligatory upon all.

My ardent desire is, and my aim has been, to comply strictly with all our engagements, foreign and domestic; but to keep the United

States free from political connections with every other country, to see them independent of all and under the influence of none.

The name of American, which belongs to you in your national capacity, must always exalt the just pride of patriotism more than any appellation derived from local discriminations. With slight shades of difference, you have the same religion, manners, habits and political principles. You have in common cause fought and triumphed together.

Guard against the postures of pretended patriotism.

My first wish is to see this plague to mankind banished from off the earth, and the sons and daughters of this world employed in more pleasing and innocent amusements, than in preparing implements and exercising them for the destruction of mankind.
(on war)

I hope I shall possess firmness and virtue enough to maintain what I consider the most enviable of all titles, the character of an honest man.

It is substantially true, that virtue or morality is a necessary spring of popular government.

As a very important source of strength and security, cherish public credit. One method of preserving it is to use it as sparingly as possible.

When we assumed the soldier, we did not lay aside the citizen.

Of all the animosities which have existed among mankind, those which are caused by a difference of sentiments in religion appear to be the most inveterate and distressing, and ought most to be deprecated.

Associate yourself with men of good quality if you esteem your own reputation; for 'tis better to be alone than in bad company.

Few men have virtue to withstand the highest bidder.

I do not mean to exclude altogether the idea of patriotism, I know it exists, and I know it has done much in the present contest. But I will venture to assert, that a great and lasting war can never be supported on this principle alone. It must be aided by a prospect of interest, or some reward.

Labor to keep alive in your breast that little spark of celestial fire called Conscience.

How pitiful in the eyes of reason is that false ambition which desolates the world with fire and sword for the purposes of conquest and fame, when compared to the milder virtues of making our neighbors and our fellow men as happy as their frail conditions and perishable natures permit them to be.

There is not a man living who wishes more sincerely than I do to see a plan adopted for the abolition of it [slavery]. But there is only one proper way and effectual mode by which it can be accomplished, and that is by legislative authority; and for this, as far as my suffrage will go, shall never be wanting.

Be courteous to all, but intimate with few, and let those few be well tried before you give them your confidence.

I long ago despaired of any other reward for my services than the satisfaction arising from a consciousness of doing my duty, and from the esteem of my friends.

'Tis well.
(*his last words*)

☆ JOHN ADAMS ☆

2nd President

Birth: October 30, 1735   Death: July 4, 1826
Term: March 4, 1797–March 3, 1801

THE ADAMS (JOHN) PRESIDENCY

• *Navy Department and Marine Corps created (1798)*

• *Capital moved to Washington, D.C. (1800)*

• *Library of Congress established (1800)*

It is generally conceded that it was John Adams's good fortune to have pursued the presidency in the 1790s and not in the televised elections of the 1990s. Adams was short, portly, and talked with a lisp; he was hot tempered and moody; his hands shook with palsy; and toothless, he refused to wear dentures.

Born in Quincy, Massachusetts, and educated at Harvard, Adams was the first in a long line of presidential lawyers. He was admitted to the bar in 1758, and his practice is best remembered for two cases: his successful defense of John Hancock for having smuggled wine into Boston without paying proper duty; and his courageous and unpopular defense of the British soldiers charged with perpetrating the Boston Massacre.

After having served in the Massachusetts legislature from 1770 to 1774, Adams was elected as a delegate to the Continental Congress, where he led the debate to have the Declaration of Independence passed. He and Thomas Jefferson are the only presidents to have signed the Declaration of Independence.

He next served the new nation as a diplomat to the Netherlands (from which he secured loans, a process that caused him to liken the Dutch to "a school of sharks") and France (where he experienced little success, in great part because of his Puritan disdain for the sexual adventures of his popular fellow diplomat, Benjamin Franklin).

On October 25, 1764, then age twenty-eight, Adams married Abigail Smith, nineteen (over the objections of the bride's mother, who was appalled that a member of her distinguished family would throw her life away on a country lawyer). Adams first took a romantic interest in Abigail when she was seventeen, shy, and always, seemingly, in the midst of reading a book. She surprised Adams with her knowledge and love of poetry, philosophy, and politics, especially since she was denied all formal education because her parents considered academic pursuits inappropriate training for a wife.

Upon the election of George Washington as president, Adams became vice president, a job he disdained for its requirement that he be quiet while others talked . . .

My country has in its wisdom contrived for me the most insignificant office that ever the invention of man contrived or his imagination conceived.

In the election of 1796—the nation's first real presidential campaign—Adams and his opponent, Thomas Jefferson, established the tone and tenor for all future national elections: the campaign staffs of both worked devotedly at smearing the opposition. Adams was described as a despot, distrustful of the public and longing for an American monarchy. Jefferson, on the other hand, was charged with being a demagogue, preying on people's fears simply to further his own selfish political fortunes. Adams's campaign urged voters to choose "God—and a religious President" over "Jefferson . . . and no God" and further warned that if Jefferson were elected, "murder, robbery, rape, adultery, and incest will be openly taught and practiced."

Adams was the first president to live in the new capital city of Washington, D.C., and the first to occupy the White House. Only six rooms were ready when he moved in with Abigail, who hung the family laundry in the empty East Room.

Adams's presidency was dominated by the war between France and England. Many urged the United States to have close ties with England even if it meant war with France. But Adams resolutely held that the United States should not be closely tied with any European country; nor should such a young nation be involved in a draining, perhaps enduring, war. Adams did, however, establish a navy and although there was no formal declaration of war, American and French warships fought whenever they met. Adams eventually sent a team of peace negotiators to France (which attempted to charge the United States a fee of $250,000 just for the privilege of a conversation). This decision to pursue peace with France probably cost Adams his reelection.

He returned to his home in Massachusetts and for the next twenty-five years fed his insatiable curiosity, reading new books, rereading the classics, and enjoying much correspondence. Adams even buried his differences with Thomas Jefferson and, in a flurry of letters, rekindled the friendship they had enjoyed during the Revolution.

In 1825, he enjoyed an opportunity denied to every other President—to see his son, John Quincy Adams, elected president.

In a most remarkable coincidence, Adams and Jefferson both died on July 4, 1826 (Jefferson, a few hours before Adams). Thus the only two signers of the Declaration of Independence to become president passed away simultaneously, on the fiftieth anniversary of its adoption.

Yesterday the greatest question was decided, which ever was debated in America, and a greater perhaps never was nor will be decided among men. A resolution was passed without one dissenting colony "that these United Colonies are, and of right ought to be, free and independent states."
(July 3, 1776)

I pray Heaven to bestow the best of blessings on this house and all that shall hereafter inhabit it. May none but honest and wise men ever rule under this roof.
(written shortly after moving into the new White House as the second president)

I must study politics and war that my sons may have liberty to study mathematics and philosophy.

I do not say when I became a politician, for that I never was.

Let the human mind loose. It must be loosed; it will be loose. Superstition and despotism cannot confine it.

He is too illiterate, unread, unlearned for his station and reputation.
(on George Washington)

No man who ever held the office of President would congratulate a friend on obtaining it. He will make one man ungrateful, and a hundred men his enemies, for every office he can bestow.

Here lies John Adams, who took upon himself the responsibility of peace with France in the year 1800.
(suggested epitaph for himself)

Ambition is the subtlest Beast of the Intellectual and Moral Field. It is wonderfully adroit in concealing itself from its owner.

America is a great, unwieldy body. Its progress must be slow. It is like a large fleet sailing under convoy. The fleetist sailers [sic] must wait for the dullest and slowest.

Did you ever see a portrait of a great man without perceiving strong traits of pain and anxiety?

I have accepted a seat in the House of Representatives, and thereby have consented to my own ruin, to your ruin, and the ruin of our children. I give you this warning, that you may prepare your mind for your fate.
(*to Abigail Adams*)

The business of the Congress is tedious beyond expression. . . . Every man in it is a great man, an orator, a critic, a statesman; and therefore every man upon every question must show his oratory, his criticism, and his political abilities.

As much as I converse with sages and heroes, they have very little of my love and admiration. I long for rural and domestic scenes, for the warbling of birds and the prattling of my children.

The body politic is . . . a social compact, by which the whole people covenants with each citizen, and each citizen with the whole people, that all shall be governed by certain laws for the common good.
(*on the Constitution*)

I could never do anything but was ascribed to sinister motives.

When annual elections end, there slavery begins.

You will never be alone with a poet in your pocket.

I agree with you that in politics the middle way is none at all.

The preservation of the means of knowledge among the lowest ranks is of more importance to the public than all the property of all the rich men in the country.
(on education)

While all other sciences advanced, that of government is at a standstill—little better understood, little better practiced now than three or four thousand years ago.

Liberty, according to my metaphysics, is an intellectual quality; an attribute that belongs not to fate nor chance.

The balance of power in a society accompanies the balance of property in land.

I have lived in this old and frail tenement a great many years; it is very much dilapidated; and, from all that I can learn, my landlord doesn't intend to repair it.
(on his aging body)

☆ THOMAS JEFFERSON ☆

3rd President

Birth: April 13, 1743   Death: July 4, 1826
Term: March 4, 1801–March 3, 1809

THE JEFFERSON PRESIDENCY

- *Establishment of United States Military Academy authorized (1802)*

- *Louisiana Purchase (1803)*

- *Ohio admitted as seventeenth state (1803)*

- *The wine bill for this eight-year presidency: $10,000*

A true Renaissance man, Thomas Jefferson's greatest interests included architecture, interior design, music, inventing, languages, law, mathematics, botany, animal husbandry, meteorology, writing, reading, politics, mechanical engineering, and marijuana cultivation (he maintained an acre on the grounds of Monticello, his beloved hilltop mansion). Regretfully, plans to include a billiard room in the dome of the house were quashed when, before Monticello could even be completed, the state of Virginia outlawed billiards.

Jefferson was only twenty-six when he was elected to the Virginia legislature. A poor public speaker, he exerted his influence through prolific writing (he wrote standing up) of letters and articles. His opinions often focused on the increasing troubles between the American Colonies and Great Britain. One such opinion piece, "The Rights of America," caused his name to become known

14

throughout the Colonies (and England, where he was declared a traitor to be hanged at once if seized).

Because of his fame as a writer, he was appointed to write the Declaration of Independence. From June 11 to 28, 1776, Jefferson composed the founding document of the Revolution unaided by any reference sources. His guiding purpose, he explained years later, was

> not to find new principles, or new arguments, never before thought of, not merely to say things which had never been said before; but to place before mankind the common sense of the subject, in terms so plain and firm as to command their assent.

At age twenty-eight, he married Martha Wayles Skelton, to whom he was exclusively devoted throughout their ten-year marriage. Just months after giving birth to their seventh child, she died. Jefferson kept his promise to Martha, on her deathbed, never to remarry. Inconsolable upon her death, he refused to leave his room for three weeks.

Prior to the presidency, Jefferson served in the Virginia House of Delegates, as governor of Virginia, as a member of the Continental Congress, as a minister to France, as the nation's first secretary of state, and as vice president during the presidency of John Adams.

Jefferson's inauguration was held in Washington, D.C., on March 4, 1801. The most significant achievement of his administration was the Louisiana Purchase in 1803. For $15 million—or only 3¢ an acre—the United States purchased from France a vast region between the Mississippi River and the Rocky Mountains, which now makes up all or part of fifteen states.

Eager to learn more about the West, Jefferson commissioned Meriwether Lewis and William Clark to lead an expedition of exploration. Their published observations gathered over the two-and-a-half-year, 8,000-mile trek provided the government, scholars, and the public with much fresh and vital information.

Jefferson also signed, in 1807, a bill that banned the importing of slaves into the United States and its territories (although some continued to be smuggled in until the Civil War).

His presidency ended two years later and he entered a retirement full of activity, encumbered with vast debts. To the federal government, he sold his extensive personal library, which then served as the core collection of the new Library of Congress. He also founded the University of Virginia.

Jefferson died the same day as his presidential predecessor, John Adams—July 4, 1826, the fiftieth anniversary of the adoption of the Declaration of Independence. He was buried in a simple ceremony on the grounds of Monticello, at the base of a tombstone with an inscription he himself had authored:

Here was buried Thomas Jefferson,
Author of the Declaration of Independence,
of the Statute of Virginia for Religious Freedom, and
the Father of the University of Virginia.

Jefferson's will instructed that certain slaves be freed, including those who were rumored to be his children.

☆　☆　☆

When in the course of human events, it becomes necessary for one person to dissolve the political bands which have connected them with another, and to assume among the powers of the earth the separate and equal station to which the Laws of Nature and of Nature's God entitle them, a decent respect to the opinions of

mankind requires that they should declare the causes which impel them to the separation . . .
(*from the Declaration of Independence*)

We hold these truths to be self-evident, that all men are created equal, that they are endowed by their Creator with certain unalienable Rights, that among these are Life, Liberty and the pursuit of Happiness. That to secure these rights, Governments are instituted among Men, deriving their just powers from the consent of the governed. That whenever any Form of Government becomes destructive to those ends, it is the Right of the People to alter or abolish it and to institute a new Government, laying its foundation on such principles and organizing its power in such form, as to them shall seem most likely to effect their Safety and Happiness.
(*from the Declaration of Independence*)

Rebellion to Tyrants is Obedience to God.

A bill of rights is what the people are entitled to against every government on earth, general or particular; and what no just government should refuse, or rest on inference.

Whenever you are to do a thing, though it can never be known but to yourself, ask yourself how you would act were all the world looking at you, and act accordingly.

The moral sense, or conscience, is as much a part of man as his leg or arm. It is given to all human beings in a stronger or weaker degree, as force of members is given them in a greater or less degree.

Bear in mind this sacred principle, that though the will of the majority is in all cases to prevail, that will to be rightful must be reasonable; that the minority possess their equal rights, which equal law must protect, and to violate would be oppression.

Science is my passion, politics my duty.

Question with boldness even the existence of God; because, if there be one, he must more approve of the homage of reason than that of blindfolded fear.

I view great cities as pestilential to the morals, the health, and the liberties of man.

A little rebellion now and then is a good thing, and as necessary in the political world as storms in the physical.

He was incapable of fear, meeting personal dangers with the calmest unconcern. Perhaps the strongest feature in his character was prudence, never acting until every circumstance, every consideration, was maturely weighed. . . . His integrity was most pure, his justice the most inflexible I have ever known, no motives of interest or consanguinity, of friendship, or hatred, being able to bias his decision. He was, indeed, in every sense of the words, a wise, a good, and a great man.
(on George Washington)

He is distrustful, obstinate, excessively vain, and takes no counsel from anyone.
(on John Adams)

I feel much alarmed at the prospect of seeing General [Andrew] Jackson President. He is one of the most unfit men I know for such a place.

No man has a natural right to commit aggression on the equal rights of another; and this is all from which the laws ought to restrain him.

I think our governments will remain virtuous for many centuries; as long as they remain chiefly agricultural; and this will be as long as there shall be vacant lands in any part of America. When they get piled upon one another in large cities, as in Europe, they will become corrupt as in Europe, and go to eating one another as they do there.

No occupation is so delightful to me as the culture of the earth.

Its soul, its climate, its equality, liberty, laws, people, and manners. My god! how little do my countrymen know what precious blessings they are in possession of, and which no other people on earth enjoy!

Were we to act but in cases where no contrary opinion of a lawyer can be had, we should never act.

That one hundred and fifty lawyers should do business together is not to be expected.

Whenever a man has cast a longing eye on offices, a rottenness begins in his conduct.

None but an armed nation can dispense with a standing army.

I sincerely believe that banking establishments are more dangerous than standing armies, and that the principle of spending money to be paid by posterity, under the name of funding, is but swindling futurity on a large scale.

I think we have more machinery of government than is necessary, too many parasites living on the labor of the industrious.

The earth belongs to the living, not the dead.

He is happiest of whom the world says least, good or bad.

I laid it down as a law to myself, to take no notice of the thousand calumnies issued against me, but to trust my own conduct, and the good sense and candor of my fellow citizens.

Some men look at constitutions with sanctimonious reverence, and deem them like the Ark of the Covenant, too sacred to be touched. They ascribe to the men of the preceding age a wisdom more than human, and suppose what they did to be beyond amendment.

The time to guard against corruption and tyranny is before they shall have gotten hold of us. It is better to keep the wolf out of the fold than to trust to drawing his teeth and talons after he shall have entered.

Defamation is becoming a necessity of life; inasmuch as a dish of tea in the morning or evening cannot be digested without that stimulant.

Books constitute capital. A library book lasts as long as a house, for hundreds of years. It is not, then, an article of mere consumption but fairly of capital, and often in the case of professional men, setting out in life, it is their only capital.

Great innovations should not be forced on slender majorities.

I like the dreams of the future better than the history of the past.

The government is best that governs least.

Happiness is not being pained in body or troubled in mind.

Honesty is the first chapter in the book of wisdom.

There is a fullness of time when men should go, and not occupy too long the ground to which others have a right to advance.
(*on death*)

The republican is the only form of government which is not eternally at open or secret war with the rights of mankind.

I know no safe depository of the ultimate powers of society but the people themselves; and if we think them not enlightened enough to exercise their control with a wholesome discretion, the remedy is not to take it from them, but to inform their discretion by education.

Humble as I am, plebeian as I may be deemed, permit me in the presence of this brilliant assemblage to enunciate the truth that courts and cabinets, the President and his advisers, derive their power and their greatness from the people.

Peace, commerce, and honest friendship with all nations, entangling alliances with none.

The less we have to do with the amities or enmities of Europe the better. Not in our day, but at no distant one, we may shake a rod over the heads of all, which may make the stoutest tremble. But I hope our wisdom will grow without power, and teach us, that the less we use our power the greatest it will be.

Some ladies think they may, under the privileges of the deshabille, be loose and negligent of their dress in the morning. But be you, from the moment you rise till you go to bed, as cleanly and properly dressed as at the hours of dinner or tea.
(to his daughter Martha, age eleven)

I wish to see this beverage become common instead of the whiskey which kills one-third of our citizens and ruins their families.
(on beer)

The opinions of men are not the object of civil government, nor under its jurisdiction.

An injured friend is the bitterest of foes.

The will of the people is the only legitimate foundation of any government, and to protect its free expression should be our first object.

A wise and frugal government, which shall restrain men from injuring one another, shall leave them otherwise free to regulate their own pursuits of industry and improvement, and shall not take from the mouth of labor the bread it has earned. This is the sum of good government . . .

If the happiness of the mass of the people can be secured at the expense of a little tempest now and then or even of a little blood, it will be a precious purchase.

It is neither wealth nor splendor, but tranquillity and occupation, which give happiness.

The new circumstances under which we are placed call for new words, new phrases, and for the transfer of old words to new objects. An American dialect will therefore be formed.

I find the pain of a little censure, even when it is unfounded, is more acute than the pleasure of much praise.

General Washington set the example of voluntary retirement after eight years. I shall follow it. And a few more precedents will oppose the obstacle of habit to anyone who after a while shall endeavor to extend his term.

It is incumbent on every generation to pay its own debts as it goes—a principle which, if acted on, would save one-half the wars of the world.

A pirate spreading misery and ruin over the face of the ocean. *(on Great Britain)*

In matters of principle, stand like a rock; in matters of taste, swim with the current.

The hole and the patch should be commensurate.

If thinking men would have the courage to think for themselves, and to speak what they think, it would be found they do not differ in religious opinion as much as is supposed.

My idea is that we should be made one nation in every case concerning foreign affairs, and separate ones in whatever is merely domestic.
(on the states)

It is error alone which needs the support of the government. Truth can stand by itself.

The tree of liberty must be refreshed from time to time with the blood of patriots and tyrants.

Whatever enables us to go to war, secures our peace.

The foundation on which all [our constitutions] are built is the natural equality of man, the denial of every preeminence but that annexed to legal office, and particularly the denial of a preeminence by birth.

Force cannot give right.

History, in general, only informs us what bad government is.

The natural progress of things is for liberty to yield and government to gain ground.

It behooves every man who values liberty of conscience for himself, to resist invasions of it in the case of others.

The bulk of mankind are schoolboys through life.

No man will ever bring out of the Presidency the reputation which carries him into it.

Is uniformity obtainable? Millions of innocent men, women and children, since the introduction of Christianity have been burnt, tortured, fined, imprisoned; yet we have not advanced an inch toward uniformity.

Victory and defeat are each of the same price.

When a man assumes a public trust, he should consider himself as public property.

☆ JAMES MADISON ☆

4th President

Birth: March 16, 1751   Death: June 28, 1836
Term: March 4, 1809–March 3, 1817

THE MADISON PRESIDENCY

- *War declared against England (1812)*
- *Louisiana (1812) and Indiana (1816) admitted as states*
- *Peace treaty signed with England (1814)*
- *Ice cream first served at White House*

Some president has to be the smallest. At five feet, four inches, and never more than 100 pounds, James Madison is that president.

Madison was raised on Montpelier, the family plantation in Virginia, at a time when the possibility of an Indian attack was always feared. Although no such attack ever came to Montpelier, as a child the much-overheard scenario permanently prejudiced Madison against Native Americans. (His biographer Irving Brant notes, "The boy had seen the tomahawk and torch too vividly in his mind's eye to permit him to view the Indian as anything but a savage.")

After studying under several private tutors and proving himself a dedicated student, Madison completed extensive studies—including Latin, Greek, science, geography, math, speech, debate, philosophy, and rhetoric—at Princeton University in just two years. He seriously considered becoming an Episcopalian priest; instead, chose politics, serving in the Virginia Convention, the

Virginia House of Delegates, the Council of States, the Continental Congress, the U.S. House of Representatives, and as secretary of state in the Jefferson administration.

Although Madison may have been the country's smallest president, he is also known as one of the "Big Four from Virginia" (the others being Washington, Jefferson, and Monroe) and as the "Father of the Constitution," for as a delegate to the Constitutional Convention, he drafted much of the document—arguing successfully for the creation of a strong central government, maintaining a comprehensive record of the proceedings, and marshaling public opinion in favor of its ratification.

Madison was Jefferson's choice to succeed him in office. And although many in the Northeast wanted to see a non-Virginian in the White House, Jefferson's popularity was so great that the southern and western states held firm for Madison. He secured 122 electoral votes while his opponents, Charles Cotesworth Pinckney of South Carolina and George Clinton of New York, received only 47 and 6 votes respectively.

Madison's presidency was dominated by the War of 1812 (1812–14), which had several causes including the British seizure of ships, Indian unrest—encouraged and exploited by England—and the rise of "War Hawks" such as Henry Clay and John C. Calhoun. The War Hawks considered the war an opportunity to seize Canada from England and Florida from Spain (an ally of England). Eventually, on June 1, 1812, Madison asked Congress to declare war on England. The English quickly captured Washington, D.C., where they burned the White House and the Capitol building, only to be turned back upon attacking Baltimore. It was during the battle of Baltimore that Francis Scott Key was inspired to write "The Star-Spangled Banner."

Madison began peace negotiations almost as soon as he had declared war. By December 1814, both sides were war weary enough to talk peace. The Treaty of Ghent was quickly signed.

The most important effect of the war was that it marked the

end of the economic dependence of the United States on England. The conflict had forced domestic industry to fill the vacuum created by the suspension of trade with Europe, and that industry continued to expand, driving the young nation's economy.

In 1794, at the age of forty-three, Madison married Dolley Payne Todd, twenty-six, a widow with one son. A vivacious and buxom beauty whose physical features were accentuated by the minuscule husband at her side, she charmed official Washington as few First Ladies have. When British troops advanced on the capital in 1814, she arranged for the safe transport of certain national treasures. With time running out, she had the full-length portrait of George Washington (by Gilbert Stuart), cut from its frame and taken safely away. From the White House on that very night, she wrote her sister:

> I am still here within sound of the cannon! Mr. Madison comes not; may God protect him! A wagon has been procured; I have filled it with the plate and most valuable portable articles belonging to the house.

After Madison's death, Dolley returned to Washington, where she was once again a popular figure on the official social scene. However, her spendthrift son, John Todd, caused such a severe drain on her finances that she had to sell both Madison's papers and Montpelier. She died, virtually destitute, thirteen years after her husband.

At the end of his presidency, Madison returned to Virginia, where, although he struggled financially (due in part to his stepson's extensive debts), he worked hard to abolish slavery and to assist Jefferson in establishing the University of Virginia.

Becoming very ill in May and June of 1836, he rejected the offer of stimulants to keep him alive until July 4 so that he might become the fourth president of the first five presidents to have died on the same date (his successor at the White House, James Monroe, had died on July 4, 1831).

His last words, just as he expired, were: "Nothing more than a change of mind."

Since the general civilization of mankind, I believe there are more instances of the abridgment of the freedom of the people by gradual and silent encroachments of those in power than by violent and sudden usurpations.

I flung forward the flag of the country, sure that the people would press onward and defend it.
(on his decision to enter the War of 1812)

In a free government the security for civil rights must be the same as for religious rights. It consists in the one case in the multiplicity of interest, and in the other in the multiplicity of sects.

Having outlived so many of my contemporaries, I ought not to forget that I may be thought of to have outlived myself.

A standing army is one of the greatest mischiefs that can possibly happen.

Always remember[ing] that an armed and trained militia is the firmest bulwark of republics—that without standing armies their liberty can never be in danger, nor with large ones safe.

Conscience is the most sacred of all property . . . To guard a man's house as his castle, to pay public and enforce private debts with the most exact faith, can give no title to invade a man's conscience which is more sacred than his castle.

Every word [of the Constitution] decides a question between power and liberty.

In Europe, charters of liberty have been granted by power. America has set the example, and France has followed it, of charters of power granted by liberty.

In a democracy the people meet and exercise the government in person; in a republic, they assemble and administer it by their representatives and agents. A democracy, consequently, will be confined to a small spot. A republic may be extended over a large region.

It is to be hoped that by expressing a national disapprobation of this [slave] trade we may destroy it, and make ourselves free from reproaches, and our posterity from the imbecility ever attendant on a country filled with slaves.

Justice is the end of government. It is the end of civil society. It ever has been and ever will be pursued until it be obtained, or until liberty be lost in the pursuit.

Liberty is to faction what air is to fire, an aliment without which it instantly expires. But it could not be less folly to abolish liberty, which is essential to political life, because it nourishes faction, than it would be to wish the annihilation of air, which is essential to animal life, because it imparts to fire its destructive agency.

I go on the principle that a public debt is a public curse.

It is universally admitted that a well-instructed people alone can be permanently a free people.

The capacity of the female mind for studies of the highest order cannot be doubted, having been sufficiently illustrated by its works of genius, of erudition, and of science.

The diffusion of knowledge is the only guardian of true liberty.

It may be said of him as has been said of others that he was a "walking library," and what can be said of but few such prodigies, that a Genius of Philosophy ever walked hand in hand with him. *(on Thomas Jefferson)*

It is a melancholy reflection that liberty should be equally exposed to danger whether the Government have too much or too little power.

All power in human hands is liable to be abused.

☆ JAMES MONROE ☆

5th President

Birth: April 28, 1758   Death: July 4, 1831
Term: March 4, 1817–March 3, 1825

THE MONROE PRESIDENCY

- *Mississippi (1817), Illinois (1818), Alabama (1818), Maine (1820), and Missouri (1821) admitted as states*

- *Florida purchased from Spain (1819)*

- *Monroe Doctrine proclaimed (1823)*

While a student at William and Mary College, James Monroe and others raided the arsenal at the governor's palace, stealing two hundred muskets and three hundred swords to help arm the Williamsburg militia. The next year, Monroe dropped out of college to join Washington's army.

Monroe was born in Virginia, where his father was a prominent and successful planter. When the elder Monroe died, James, at age sixteen, inherited his father's entire estate and assumed responsibility for his three younger brothers.

Monroe was the last of the Revolutionary leaders to become president. He crossed the Delaware with Washington and fought at Brandywine, Germantown, and Monmouth. At Trenton, a bullet struck him and remained in his shoulder for the rest of his life.

Although he failed to return to college after the war to earn a degree, he fared quite well, studying law under no less an expert than Thomas Jefferson.

At twenty-eight, Monroe married Elizabeth Kortright, seventeen, the daughter of a wealthy New York merchant. In personal matters, he was often dominated by his wife and their two elegant daughters, who put on rather aristocratic airs. Although it would have been difficult for almost anyone to follow the popular social reign of Dolley Madison, the Monroe women were known as notorious snobs. Monroe's wife and two daughters spent his money so freely that he found himself in serious financial difficulty at the time of his death.

With Jefferson's encouragement and sponsorship, Monroe turned to a career in politics, serving in the Virginia Assembly, the Continental Congress, and the U.S. Senate. He also served as minister to France, governor of Virginia, minister to Great Britain, and as both secretary of state and secretary of war in the Madison administration. He had the ideal preparation to claim his eventual great success in the area of foreign policy.

Monroe's Republican nomination for the presidency in 1816 was essentially tantamount to election, for the Federalist party's opposition to the War of 1812 had left it moribund and powerless. Monroe faced even less of a challenge upon his reelection in 1821.

The Monroe administration became known as the "era of good feelings," for this was a brief and unusual period in America's history when a single party commanded the affections of virtually all of the country's various social segments.

Responding to concerns that Spain might attempt to recapture its former colonies in Latin America and that Russia might extend its claims in Alaska to include the Oregon territory, Monroe delivered a message to Congress warning the European powers against intervention in the Western Hemisphere. This is the message that came to be known as the Monroe Doctrine. It has been a basic doctrine of the United States ever since.

After six years of retirement, Monroe died on July 4, 1831, while visiting his daughter in New York City. He thus became the third president to die on that date (Washington didn't know any better, and Madison didn't even try).

☆　☆　☆

In contemplating what we still have to perform, the heart of every citizen must expand with joy when he reflects how near our Government has approached to perfection . . .

The American continents . . . are henceforth not to be considered as subjects for future colonization by any European powers. (*the Monroe Doctrine*)

We find that brevity is a characteristic of the instrument [the Constitution].

A complete remedy to a political disease is seldom found until something like a crisis occurs, and this is promoted by the abuse of those who have rendered the most important services, and whose characters will bear the test of enquiry.

Our great resources therefore remain untouched for any purpose which may affect the vital interest of the nation. For all such purposes they are inexhaustible. They are more especially to be found in the virtue, patriotism and intelligence of our fellow-citizens, and in the devotion with which they would yield up by any just measure of taxation all their property in support of the rights and honor of their country.

The progress of our settlements westward, supported as they are by a dense population, has constantly driven them [Native Americans] back, with almost the total sacrifice of the lands which they have been compelled to abandon. They have claims on the magnanimity and, I may add, on the justice of this nation which we must all feel.

In this great nation there is but one order, that of the people, whose power, by a peculiarly happy improvement of the representative principle, is transferred from them, without impairing in the slightest degree their sovereignty, to bodies of their own creation, and to persons elected by themselves, in the full extent necessary for the purposes of free, enlightened, and efficient government.

Preparation for war is a constant stimulus to suspicion and ill will.

Mrs. Monroe hath added a daughter to our society who tho' noisy, contributes greatly to its amusement.
(letter to Thomas Jefferson regarding the birth of his daughter)

If America wants concessions, she must fight for them. We must purchase our power with our blood.

☆ JOHN QUINCY ADAMS ☆

6th President

Birth: July 11, 1767   Death: February 23, 1848
Term: March 4, 1825–March 3, 1829

THE ADAMS (JOHN QUINCY) PRESIDENCY

• *Erie Canal opens (1825)*

• *Baltimore & Ohio railroad construction begins (1827)*

• *President goes skinny-dipping in the Potomac*

John Quincy Adams was the only son of a president to become president. His father was John Adams. And like his father, John Quincy was no "life of the party," suffering from insomnia, indigestion, anxiety, eye discomfort, and serious bouts of mental depression—what he himself called "uncontrollable dejection of spirits" and "a sluggish carelessness of life" with "an imaginary wish that life were terminated." He described himself as "a man of reserved, cold, and forbidding manners." And, like many Bostonians, he was notoriously careless about his dress, having at one point worn the same hat for ten years.

Born a child of the American Revolution, he witnessed the Battle of Bunker Hill at age eight. With his father often away working on revolutionary matters, John Quincy took seriously his responsibilities as the man of the family. At age fourteen, he traveled in Europe and Russia, often alone, through Helsinki, Stockholm, St. Petersburg, Amsterdam, Hamburg, and Copenhagen. When he was fifteen, he was serving as his father's secretary—at the very time John Adams was writing the peace treaty that ended the American Revolution.

At the war's end, John Quincy returned to America to study law at Harvard. But before his practice had hardly begun, George Washington appointed him minister to the Netherlands. He went on to serve as minister to Prussia, as Massachusetts state senator, U.S. senator, minister to Russia, chief negotiator for the Treaty of Ghent (to end the War of 1812), minister to Great Britain, and secretary of state for President Monroe.

In 1797, at age thirty, he married an Englishwoman (she would become the only foreign-born First Lady), Louisa Catherine Johnson, age twenty-two. Mrs. Adams eventually became reclusive and depressed. She mourned the untimely death of her two oldest sons and regretted ever having married into the Adams family, the men of which she found cold and insensitive. On their fourteenth anniversary, Adams said of their marriage:

> Our union has not been without its trials, its many differences of sentiment, of tastes, and of opinions in regard to domestic economy, and to the education of children.

In 1824, Adams ran for the presidency against Andrew Jackson, William H. Crawford, and Henry Clay. During these years, because the nominating caucus had fallen into disrepute, the presidential candidates came forward on the basis of regional endorsements. No party labels were used. Although his presidential credentials were beyond question, Adams's personality was not, especially when matched against the extremely popular and gregarious Andrew Jackson. None of the candidates received a majority of the electoral vote, however, and the election was thrown to the House of Representatives. Adams was chosen, even though Jackson had won by nearly 35,000 in the popular vote. Four years later, Adams lost to Jackson in a bid for reelection.

Adams was the first president to endorse federally sponsored internal improvements such as roads, canals, a national university, and an astronomical observatory. These efforts often resulted in clashes with Congress, however, eventually weakening the effectiveness of his presidency.

Every warm morning during his term in office, Adams would slip down to the Potomac for a quick dip in the buff. Once a reporter, Anne Royall, surprised him during his swim, sat down on his clothes, and refused to go away until he had given her an interview he had been trying to avoid.

After his reelection defeat, he returned to Massachusetts and was elected to the U.S. House of Representatives, where he served for the next seventeen years. Some assumed he would regard serving in Congress as a disgrace after having been president. His response was true to form: no man was ever disgraced by serving his country. He is the only former president to have served in Congress.

Adams died in 1848 after suffering a stroke in the Capitol Building. His last words: "This is the end of Earth; I am content."

☆ ☆ ☆

I am a man of reserved, cold, austere, and forbidding manners; my political adversaries say, a gloomy misanthropist, and my personal enemies, an unsocial savage.
(*from his diary*)

Tyler is a political sectarian of the slave-driving, Virginian, Jeffersonian school, principled against all improvement, with all the interests and passions and vices of slavery rooted in his moral and political constitution.
(*on John Tyler*)

With most men reform is a trade. . . . Reform for its own sake seldom thrives.

There is in the clergy of all the Christian denominations a time-serving, cringing, subservient morality, as wide from the spirit of the Gospel as it is from the intrepid assertion and vindication of truth.

Whether to the nation or to the State, no service can or ever will be rendered by a more able or a more faithful public servant.
(on Millard Fillmore)

Wherever the standard of freedom and independence has been or shall be unfurled, there will be America's heart, her benedictions and her prayers. But she does not go abroad in search of monsters to destroy. She is the champion and vindicator only of her own.

Our Constitution professedly rests upon the good sense and attachment of the people. This basis, weak as it may appear, has not yet been found to fail.

The prosperity of the country, independent of all agency of the Government, is so great that the people have nothing to disturb them but their own waywardness and corruption.

The only temper that honors a nation is that which rises in proportion to the pressure upon it.

I could go into it [retirement] with a combination of parties and of public men against my character and reputation such as I believe never before was exhibited against any man since this Union existed.

America, with the same voice which spoke herself into existence as a nation, proclaimed to mankind the inextinguishable rights of human nature, and the only lawful foundation of government.

The great problem of legislation is, so to organize the civil government of a community . . . that in the operation of human institutions upon social action, self-love and social may be made the same.

Individual liberty is individual power, and as the power of a community is a mass compounded of individual powers, the nation which enjoys the most freedom must necessarily be in proportion to its numbers the most powerful nation.

To furnish the means of acquiring knowledge is . . . the greatest benefit that can be conferred upon mankind. It prolongs life itself and enlarges the sphere of existence.
(*report on the establishment of the Smithsonian Institution*)

[Journalists] are a sort of assassins who sit with loaded blunderbusses at the corners of streets and fire them off for hire or for sport at any passenger they select.

Literature has been the charm of my life, and, could I have carved out my own fortunes, to literature would my whole life have been devoted.

I want (who does not want?) a wife
　Affectionate and fair,
To solace all the woes of life
　And all its days to share;
Of temper sweet, of yielding will,
　Of firm yet placid mind,
With all my faults to love me still,
　With sentiments refined.
—"The Wants of Man," c. 1787

Slavery is the great and foul stain upon the North American Union, and it is a contemplation worthy of the most exalted soul whether its total abolition is or is not practicable.

Why does it follow that women are fitted for nothing but the cares of domestic life, for bearing children and cooking the food of the family? . . . I say women exhibit the most exalted virtue when they depart from the domestic circle and enter on the concerns of their country, of humanity, and of their God!

All that I am my mother made me.

Independence forever!
(*on his deathbed*)

☆ ANDREW JACKSON ☆

7th President

Birth: March 15, 1767   Death: June 8, 1845
Term: March 4, 1829–March 3, 1837

THE JACKSON PRESIDENCY

- *Twenty thousand Jackson fans jam the White House on Inauguration Day (1829)*

- *A bullet is removed from the president, the result of a brawl twenty years earlier (1832)*

- *Arkansas (1836) and Michigan (1837) admitted as states*

Andrew Jackson was probably an illegal president. It seems that he was not born on American soil (as one must be, to be eligible for the presidency) but instead on a ship bound for America from Ireland.

Jackson's childhood was not an easy one. His father died just weeks before his birth. Then he developed the peculiar and life-long habit of drooling. At age fourteen, while fighting in the Revolutionary War, he was captured and severely stabbed with a saber for refusing to shine a British officer's boots (he is the only president ever to have been a prisoner of war). Worse yet, he lost his mother and both brothers during the war. At age fifteen, he was, indeed, utterly alone.

A less-than-average student, Jackson failed to pursue the Presbyterian ministry as his mother had hoped. Instead, he became a gambling, hard-drinking, woman-chasing lawyer (admitted to the North Carolina bar in 1787). One year, as chairperson of the annual Christmas ball in Salisbury, North Carolina, he sent, for laughs, formal invitations to two prostitutes, a mother-and-daughter team well known in Salisbury. The community was not amused.

Because Jackson, an attorney, mistook a preliminary divorce document as a final divorce decree, he illegally "married" Rachel Donelson Robards, the wife of Lewis Robards, in August 1791.

Robards then sued for divorce on grounds of adultery. Although the Jacksons later married legally, this initial mistake was to be used thereafter by his political foes. As Jackson moved closer to the White House, Rachel's "adultery" went national in the press. Her embarrassment and anguish resulted in depression and an illness that led to her untimely death in 1828. Jackson's fury was evident at her burial:

> In the presence of this dear saint, I can and do forgive my enemies. But those vile wretches who have slandered her must look to God for mercy.

Jackson began his political career as a public prosecutor in North Carolina. He then served as a U.S. congressman, a U.S. senator, and justice of the Tennessee Superior Court.

When in 1813, the people of Tennessee raised an army to fight the Creek Indians, Jackson was elected general. Although he had no military training, he proved to be an excellent commanding officer. The next year, after having been commissioned a general in the federal army, he soundly defeated the British at New Orleans and became a national hero.

He lost the presidential election of 1824 to John Quincy Adams, then won both the 1828 and 1832 elections as a Democrat. Jackson was sworn into office while still mourning the death of his wife. And although no formal festivities had been planned, twenty thousand jammed into the White House, destroying rugs, furniture, and glassware.

Because he was upset with how the wives of his Cabinet members treated one another, Jackson simply abandoned regular Cabinet meetings and instead began developing and directing policy with a team of informal advisers in the White House. This core group of loyalists became known at the "Kitchen Cabinet."

Jackson vetoed far more bills than any previous president (none was overridden by Congress). Most of these vetoes involved "internal improvement" bills for building roads or improving harbors.

After attending the inauguration of his handpicked successor, Martin Van Buren, Jackson retired to his 1,200-acre plantation, the Hermitage, in Tennessee. His hopes for a peaceful retirement were shattered by the need to settle the many debts of his adopted son. Jackson spent much of his remaining years in frantic efforts to avoid bankruptcy. However, he found the time to keep active in national politics, promoting the career of James K. Polk and lobbying for the annexation of Texas.

When one day in 1845 he realized that his failing health was now rapidly slipping, he gathered his friends and slaves about him and said: "I hope to meet you all in heaven. Be good children, all of you, and strive to be ready when the change comes." These were his last words.

☆ ☆ ☆

The brave man inattentive to his duty, is worth little more to his country than the coward who deserts her in the hour of danger.

No people ever lost their liberties unless they themselves first became corrupt. . . . The people are the safeguards of their own liberties, and I rely wholly on them to guard themselves.

The individual who refuses to defend his rights when called by his Government, deserves to be a slave, and must be punished as an enemy of his country and friend to her foe.

Brought up under the tyranny of Britain—although young embarked in the struggle for our liberties, in which I lost every thing that was dear to me . . . for which I have been amply repaid by living under the mild administration of a republican government. To maintain this, and the independent rights of our nation is a duty that I have ever owed to my country, to myself and posterity, and when I do all I can to support, I have only done my duty.

I cannot be intimidated from doing that which my judgment and conscience tell me is right by any earthly power.

Good officers will make good soldiers.

If you have a job in your department that can't be done by a Democrat, then abolish the job.

It is to be regretted that the rich and powerful too often bend the acts of government to their selfish purposes.

Permit me to premise, that in appointing persons to office it is not incumbent on the president to assign the reasons which govern his conduct . . . It is by his acts that he is in the respect to be judged by his constituents.

Public money is but a species of public property. It can not be raised by taxation or customs, nor brought into the Treasury in any other way except by law; but whenever and however obtained, its custody always has been and always must be, unless the Constitution be changed, intrusted to the executive department.

If our power over means is so absolute that the Supreme Court will not call into question an act of Congress . . . it becomes up to us to proceed in our legislation with the utmost caution.

You know, I never despair. I have confidence in the virtue and good sense of the people. God is just, and while we act faithfully to the Constitution, he will smile upon and prosper our exertions.

Perpetuity is stamped upon the Constitution by the blood of our Fathers.

There are, perhaps, few men who can for any length of time enjoy office and power without being more or less under the influence of feelings unfavorable to the faithful discharge of their political duties. Their integrity may be proof against improper considerations immediately addressed to themselves, but they are apt to acquire a habit of looking with indifference upon the public interests and of tolerating conduct from which an unpracticed man would revolt.

If such corruption exists in the green tree, what will be in the dry?

One man with courage makes a majority.

If a national debt is considered a national blessing, then we can get on by borrowing. But as I believe it is a national curse, my vow shall be to pay the national debt.

The moment we engage in confederations, or alliances with any nation we may from that time date the downfall of our republic.

There are no necessary evils in government. Its evils exist only in its abuses. If it would confine itself to equal protection, and, as Heaven does its rains, shower its favors alike on the high and the low, the right and the poor, it would be an unqualified blessing.

It will be my sincere and constant desire to observe toward the Indian tribes within our limits a just and liberal policy, and to give that humane and considerate attention to their rights and their wants which is consistent with the habits of our Government and the feelings of our people.

I can say with truth mine is a situation of dignified slavery.

Many of our rich men have not been content with equal protection and equal benefits, but have besought us to make them richer by act of Congress.

In a free government the demand for moral qualities should be made superior to that of talents.

I hope and trust to meet you in Heaven, both white and black— both white and black.
(on his death, to his household, including his slaves)

☆ Martin Van Buren ☆

8th President

Birth: December 5, 1782   Death: July 24, 1862
Term: March 4, 1837–March 3, 1841

THE VAN BUREN PRESIDENCY

• *Panic of 1837*

The combination of Martin Van Buren's political savvy (he organized the "Albany Regency," America's first political machine) and physical presence (slender; erect; with a high forehead; prominent, curly, red sideburns; and always dressed at the height of fashion) made him a magnet for nicknames: "Matty Van," "Old Kinderhook," "The Little Magician," "The American Talleyrand," "The Red Fox of Kinderhook," "Petticoat Pet," and after he presided over a disastrous depression, "Martin Van Ruin."

Van Buren was the first president born in the new United States; of the first seven, six were born in Colonial America and one, Jackson, probably aboard a boat en route from Ireland. Van Buren grew up in the old village of Kinderhook, New York, speaking Dutch better than English. At fourteen he took a job as a law clerk, and at twenty set up his own successful law practice.

But he was even more successful as a politician, using the state offices he held to provide jobs for friends and political supporters.

Van Buren served as a New York state senator, United States senator, governor of New York, secretary of state during Jackson's first term, and as vice president during Jackson's second term.

In 1807 he married his childhood sweetheart, Hannah Hoes.

They had four sons. In their twelfth year of marriage, she died of tuberculosis. Although seemingly devoted to his wife (he never remarried), he includes not one mention of Hannah in his autobiography.

Just two months after Van Buren's inaugural in 1837, banks in New York City suspended converting paper money into gold and silver, touching off a panic that closed banks across the country, shut down mill towns, and caused the loss of tens of thousands of jobs. Van Buren, believing that government should not interfere in private business, did little to help, and the severe economic depression continued until 1843.

The people turned on the dapper dresser and sophisticated diner, claiming he drank foreign wines and used gold forks and silver plates. His political career never recovered. In his try for reelection in 1840, Van Buren was easily defeated by William Henry Harrison; and then again—embarrassingly so—in 1848 when he ran for the presidency as the nominee of the Free Soil party (a party opposed to slavery).

In retirement, he enjoyed farming, fishing, and entertaining old friends at the family home in Kinderhook. He also toured Europe and worked on his memoirs. He died of heart failure on July 24, 1862.

☆ ☆ ☆

As to the Presidency, the two happiest days of my life were those of my entrance upon the office and my surrender of it.

He loved his country, desired to serve it, and was properly conscious of the honor of doing so.
(on John Quincy Adams)

Until the wit of man shall be able to devise some plan of representation by which all who think themselves qualified may be at the same time admitted to a participation in the Administration of its affairs, we must not expect to be relieved from the spirit of complaining, nor even surprised to find it most vehement at a period of the greatest prosperity.

I tread in the footsteps of illustrious men, whose superiors it is our happiness to believe are not found on the executive calendar of any country.

On receiving from the people the sacred trust twice confided to my illustrious predecessor [Andrew Jackson], and which he has discharged so faithfully and so well, I know that I can not expect to perform the arduous task with equal ability and success.

The capacity of the people for self-government, and their willingness, from a high sense of duty and without those exhibitions of coercive power so generally employed in other countries, . . . have also been favorably exemplified in the history of the United States.

The President is the most extraordinary man I ever saw. He does not seem to realize the vast importance of his elevation. . . . He is as tickled with the Presidency as a young man with a new bonnet. (*on William Henry Harrison*)

Most men are not scolded out of their opinion.

The people under our system, like the king in a monarchy, never dies.

Is it possible to be anything in this country without being a politician?

Ignorance and vice bred poverty which was as immutable as the seasons.

☆ WILLIAM HENRY HARRISON ☆

9th President

Birth: February 9, 1773   Death: April 4, 1841
Term: March 4, 1841–April 4, 1841

THE HARRISON (WILLIAM HENRY) PRESIDENCY

• *President quickly dies, trying to prove how healthy he is*

Although the enduring influence of his thirty-two-day presidency may be minimal, the endurance of Harrisons was not—William Henry Harrison produced far more grandchildren (48) and great-grandchildren (106) than any other president. One of those grandchildren, Benjamin Harrison, become the twenty-third president.

Born in Virginia, Harrison began premedical instruction at age fourteen. Those studies continued for several years until after his father's death, when his money was soon exhausted. He then joined the army, in August 1791.

Two years later he was fighting in the Indian wars under the direction of Major General "Mad" Anthony Wayne, who provided official commendation for Harrison's conduct and bravery in the Battle of Fallen Timbers. In 1798 he was appointed secretary of the Northwest Territory; in 1799, elected Northwest Territory delegate to the United States House of Representatives; and in 1800, appointed governor of the Indiana Territory.

In 1795, he eloped with Anna Tuthill Symmes, the daughter of a prominent frontier judge. His wife's family accepted Harrison only after he had achieved fame on the battlefield.

In 1811, the famous Indian chief Tecumseh and his followers

massed on the banks of the Tippecanoe River. Harrison led about a thousand soldiers against them. It wasn't much of a battle, but it made Harrison famous. He was given the nickname "Old Tippecanoe." When he ran for the presidency with vice presidential candidate, John Tyler, they used what proved to be a very effective slogan: "Tippecanoe and Tyler, Too."

When the War of 1812 began, Harrison was commissioned a general. His victory at the Battle of the Thames secured the Northwest and made him a national hero. He then reentered politics, serving in the U.S. House of Representatives, the Ohio Senate, and the U.S. Senate.

Harrison lost his first bid for the White House in 1836 but won four years later by a landslide over Martin Van Buren, whose presidency had been severely weakened by an economy stuck in the midst of a devastating depression.

To prove his good health, the sixty-nine-year-old Harrison (only Ronald Reagan was older upon inauguration) insisted upon riding horseback through the long inaugural parade and delivering his one-hour-and-forty-minute speech without benefit of a hat, gloves, or overcoat, even in the brisk March wind. It killed him.

He came down with a cold, which led to his death from pneumonia just weeks later. He died before his wife, who had stayed in Ohio to prepare for a late-spring arrival in Washington, had even had a chance to occupy the White House.

☆ ☆ ☆

I am the clerk of the Court of Common Pleas of Hamilton County at your service. . . . Some folks are silly enough to have formed a plan to make a President of the U.S. out of this Clerk and Clod Hopper.

We admit of no government by divine right . . . The only legitimate right to govern is an express grant of power from the governed.

A decent and manly examination of the acts of government should be not only tolerated, but encouraged.

The chains of military despotism once fastened upon a nation, ages might pass away before they could be shaken off.

But I contend that the strongest of all governments is that which is most free.

There is nothing more corrupting, nothing more destructive of the noblest and finest feelings of our nature, than the exercise of unlimited power.

☆ JOHN TYLER ☆

10th President

Birth: March 29, 1790   Death: January 18, 1862
Term: April 6, 1841–March 3, 1845

THE TYLER PRESIDENCY

- *Right of presidential succession clarified (1841)*
- *Treaty with England settles Canadian border disputes (1842)*
- *Florida admitted as state (1845)*
- *Treaty with China opens Far East trade (1844)*

When John Tyler, as an infant, once reached up his arms into the night sky to grab the shining moon, his mother was said to have remarked, "This child is destined to be a president of the United States, his wishes fly so high."

An excellent student, the Virginia-born Tyler graduated from William and Mary College at age seventeen and began the study of law under his father and his cousin, Chancellor Samuel Tyler. He was admitted to the bar in 1809.

He joined the military in 1813 and saw no action; but for this brief, uneventful service, he was awarded a veteran's land bonus of 160 acres in Iowa. He then served in the Virginia House of Delegates, as a U.S. congressman, governor of Virginia, United States senator, and vice president.

As vice president he was not kept informed of President Harrison's failing health and so was quite stunned when on April 5, 1841, he was awakened early in the morning in Williamsburg and told to rush to Washington to become president.

In 1842, at the White House, Letitia Christian, his wife of twenty-nine years and the mother of his eight children, died of a stroke. Tyler's broken heart quickly healed and while still president, the fifty-four-year-old Tyler married Julia Gardiner, twenty-three, a Washington belle with "a spectacular hourglass figure." She bore Tyler another seven children, the last when he was seventy.

Politically, though, Tyler's presidency was a lonely one. He was the first vice president to accede to the presidency, and the Constitution was ambiguous on the right of succession. Many thought Tyler should only be "acting president." He insisted, instead, that he be a full president, his powers undiminished by the manner of his accession (he returned, unopened, any mail addressed to the "Acting President"). Tyler's view ultimately prevailed, setting a precedent for the many times since when a vice president has been elevated to the presidency. Tyler was also ostracized by his own party after a series of policy conflicts with Congress (he cast nine vetoes in his one term). Even his Cabinet, which Harrison had first selected, abandoned him. He became known as "the president without a party."

Abandoned by his party and unwilling to run as a third-party candidate, Tyler did not seek reelection.

In 1840 I was called from my farm to undertake the administration of public affairs and I foresaw that I was called to a bed of thorns. I now leave that bed which has afforded me little rest, and eagerly seek repose in the quiet enjoyments of rural life.

In 1862, as he was dying, he remarked to his doctor, "I am going." "I hope not, sir," replied the doctor. "Perhaps it is best," Tyler added. Those were his last words.

Because he had supported and joined the Confederacy in his retirement (the only former president to do so), Tyler was considered a traitor in the North and no official word of his death was ever issued. Finally, in 1915, fifty years after the Civil War ended, the United States erected a memorial stone over his grave.

☆ ☆ ☆

The right to remove from office, while subjected to no just restraint, is inevitably destined to produce a spirit of crouching servility with the official corps, which in order to uphold the hand that feeds them, would lead to direct and active interference in the elections, both State and Federal.

When I was a member of either House of Congress I acted under the conviction that to *doubt* as to the constitutionality of a law was sufficient to induce me to give my vote against it; but I have not been able to bring myself to believe that a *doubtful opinion* of the [state-level] Chief Magistrate ought to outweigh the solemnly pronounced opinion of the representatives of the people and of the States.

The prudent capitalist will never adventure his capital . . . if there exists a state of uncertainty as to whether the Government will repeal tomorrow what it has enacted today.

Tippecanoe and Tyler, Too.
(Harrison-Tyler campaign)

He is a scientific Goth, resembling Alaric, destroying the country as he goes and delivering the people over to starvation. Nor does he bury his dead, but leaves them to rot on the battlefield.
(on General Grant)

Wealth can only be accumulated by the earnings of industry and the savings of frugality.

Popularity, I have always thought, may aptly be compared to a coquette—the more you woo her, the more apt is she to elude your embrace.

The great primary and controlling interest of the American people is union—union not only in the mere forms of government . . . but union founded in an attachment of . . . individuals for each other.

Patronage is the sword and cannon by which war may be made on the liberty of the human race. . . . Give the President control over the purse—the power to place the immense revenues of the country into any hands he may please, and I care not what you call him, he is "every inch a king."

If the tide of defamation and abuse shall turn, and my administration come to be praised, future Vice-Presidents who may succeed to the Presidency may feel some slight encouragement to pursue an independent course.

Here lies the body of my good horse, "The General." For twenty years he bore me around the circuit of my practice, and in all that time he never made a blunder. Would that his master could say the same!
(inscription on the grave of his horse)

☆ JAMES KNOX POLK ☆

11th President

Birth: November 2, 1795   Death: June 15, 1849
Term: March 4, 1845–March 3, 1849

THE POLK PRESIDENCY

- *Texas (1845), Iowa (1846), and Wisconsin (1848) admitted as states*
- *Treaty with England resolves Oregon boundary dispute (1846)*
- *Mexican War (1846–48)*

James K. Polk worked so hard at being a good president (a poll of historians named him the greatest one-term president) that it probably killed him.

Polk and his devoted wife worked at the White House, twelve to fourteen hours per day, up until he announced that he would retire at the end of one term:

I feel exceedingly relieved that I am now free from all public cares. I am sure I should be a happier man in my retirement than I have been during the four years I have filled the highest office in the gift of my countrymen.

Although at age forty-nine Polk was the youngest president up to that point, he literally died from exhaustion only three months after departing the White house.

Born in North Carolina, Polk moved with his family at age ten to the rough and rugged Tennessee frontier. At seventeen he found work at a store in order to learn his chosen career—merchandising. But after only a matter of weeks, he changed his mind and instead pursued a formal education which eventually led to his study of the law. In 1820 he was admitted to the bar.

He then served in the Tennessee House of Representatives and as the governor of Tennessee. At the Democratic convention of 1844 it was thought that Polk, at best, might secure a vice presidential nomination. After nine rounds of balloting among well-known candidates—including former president Martin Van Buren and future president James Buchanan—the convention swung behind Polk. He thus became the first dark-horse candidate to be nominated for president by a major party. Polk's eventual victory over Henry Clay, long a familiar figure in national politics, surprised many.

In 1824, Polk had married Sarah Childress, a lively, charming, and intelligent conversationalist. The president often conferred with her on policy matters. However, Polk's presidency wasn't much fun—Mrs. Polk, a devout Presbyterian, banned dancing and liquor in the White House. Even at the inaugural ball, in deference to the president's wife, dancing and music were halted when the Polks entered, then resumed two hours later when they left.

With his abundant energy freed from partying, Polk turned his attention to an issue that dominated his administration: the Mexican War (1846–48). The nation's victory over its southern neighbors resulted in the United States acquiring the land that eventually made up all or part of California, Nevada, Utah, Wyoming, Colorado, Texas, New Mexico, and Arizona.

After the inauguration of his successor, Zachary Taylor, in 1849, Polk immediately embarked on an extensive month-long tour of the South. He was already exhausted by his years in the White House, and the month of travel taxed his health even further. When he finally got home to Tennessee to rest, he ended up resting forever.

☆ ☆ ☆

I prefer to supervise the whole operations of the Government myself rather than entrust the public business to subordinates and this makes my duties very great.

No President who performs his duties faithfully and conscientiously can have any leisure.

The President's power is negative merely, and not affirmative.

I cannot, whilst President of the United States, descend to enter into a newspaper controversy.

I begin, more than I have ever done before, to distrust the disinterestedness and honesty of all mankind. Some selfish or local petty feeling seems to influence even members of Congress in their recommendations for office, much more than principle.

The passion for office among members of Congress is very great, if not absolutely disreputable, and greatly embarrasses the operations of the government. They create offices by their own votes and then seek to fill them themselves.

The people of the United States have no idea of the extent to which the President's time, which ought to be devoted to more important matters, is occupied by the voracious and often unprincipled persons who seek office.

In the midst of the annoyances of the herd of lazy, worthless people who come to Washington for office instead of going to work . . . I am sometimes amused at their applications. . . . One of these office seekers placed his papers of recommendation . . . No particular office was specified . . . but he answered that he thought he would be a good hand at making Treaties . . . and would like to be a minister abroad. This is about as reasonable as many other applications which are made to me.

I must have shook hands with several thousand persons . . . Some gentlemen asked me if my arm was not sore. . . . I told them that I had found that there was a great art to shaking hands . . . [I]f a man surrendered his arm to be shaken . . . he could not fail to suffer severely from it, but that if he would shake and not be shaken, grip and not be gripped, taking care always to squeeze the hand of his adversary as hard as he squeezed him that he suffered no inconvenience from it.

There is more selfishness and less principle among members of Congress . . . than I had any conception of, before I became President of the U.S.

Foreign powers do not seem to appreciate the true character of our government.

In truth, though I occupy a very high position, I am the hardest-working man in this country.

With me it is exceptionally true that the Presidency is "no bed of roses."

I am heartily rejoiced that my term is so near its close. I will soon cease to be a servant and will become a sovereign.
(on retirement)

☆ ZACHARY TAYLOR ☆

12th President

Birth: November 24, 1784   Death: July 9, 1850
Term: March 4, 1849–July 9, 1850

THE TAYLOR PRESIDENCY

- *President's faithful war horse, "Old White," grazes on the White House lawn (1849–50)*

- *Deadly cherries and iced milk served at White House (1850)*

Zachary Taylor did not "cut a dashing figure." His body was disproportionate with long, gangly arms and short, bowed legs stuck to a thick torso. He dressed comfortably, sloppily at times, often in a hodgepodge of civilian and military dress. And although he was farsighted and squinted, this dedicated tobacco chewer held the reputation for being an extremely gifted marksman when aiming at a spittoon.

A direct descendant of William Brewster, the Pilgrim leader who arrived on the *Mayflower*, Taylor was born in Virginia. A quick learner and a good student, he nonetheless received only the most basic education.

A career military officer, he served in the War of 1812 and the Black Hawk, Second Seminole, and Mexican wars. It was his victory over a much larger Mexican force at Buena Vista that made "Old Rough and Ready" (as he was affectionately known to his troops) a national hero.

The Whigs nominated Taylor for president—despite the fact that he despised politics and politicians and had never in his life cast a vote in a presidential election. Taylor was even several days late in officially acknowledging his presidential nomination, because he refused to pay the 10 cents in postage due on his formal letter of notification. In his campaign for president, Taylor said nothing, relying on a split in the opposing Democratic ranks to elect him.

In 1810 he had married Margaret "Peggy" Mackall Smith. Throughout their marriage, the hardships of following her husband from fort to fort and the birth of several children took their toll on her health. At the White House she was a semi-invalid, remaining in seclusion on the second floor and leaving the duties of official hostess to her daughter, Mrs. Betty Bliss.

Taylor's uneventful presidency lasted only sixteen months. On the Fourth of July, 1850, he attended festivities at the Washington Monument and apparently suffered sunstroke. Later that evening, he ate a large bowl of cherries and drank a pitcher of iced milk. The combination of severe sun exposure and probably tainted cherries or milk brought on such severe illness that he died four days later. His last words:

> I am about to die. I expect the summons very soon. I have tried to discharge my duties faithfully. I regret nothing, but I am sorry that I am about to leave my friends.

☆ ☆ ☆

The idea that I should become President seems to me too visionary to require a serious answer. It has never entered my head, nor is it likely to enter the head of any other person.
(*two years prior to his nomination for president*)

The power given by the Constitution to the Executive to interpose his veto is a high conservative power; but in my opinion it should never be exercised except in cases of clear violation of the Constitution, or manifest haste and want of due consideration by Congress.

For more than half a century, during which kingdoms and empires have fallen, this Union has stood unshaken. The patriots who formed it have long since descended to the grave; yet still it remains, the proudest monument to their memory. . . . In my judgment, its dissolution would be the greatest of calamities. . . . Upon its preservation must depend our own happiness and that of countless generations to come. Whatever dangers may threaten it, I shall stand by it and maintain it in its integrity to the full extent of the obligations imposed and the power conferred upon me by the Constitution.

[Farming] affords nothing sufficiently interesting to trouble my friends by communicating with them on the subject.

The axe, pick, saw & trowel, has become more the implement of the American soldier than the cannon, musket or sword.

A military education will be but of little service . . . unless practice be blended with theory.

Tell him to go to hell.
(reply to Mexican General Santa Anna's demand for surrender)

It would be judicious to act with magnanimity towards a prostrate foe.

You have fought the good fight, but you cannot make a stand.
(to his doctors on his deathbed)

☆ MILLARD FILLMORE ☆

13th President

Birth: January 7, 1800   Death: March 8, 1874
Term: July 10, 1850–March 3, 1853

THE FILLMORE PRESIDENCY

- *California admitted as state (1850)*
- *White House library established (1850–53)*

As president, Millard Fillmore stepped into an odoriferous dispute between American business and the Peruvian government regarding the control of fowl excrement, and he successfully negotiated a special treaty. Because of those efforts, American businessmen continued to secure the massive profits to be made in the guano reserves (which could be turned into valuable fertilizer) offshore of Peru.

Born in a log cabin in the Finger Lakes area of New York, Fillmore first attended school at age eighteen, surrounded by seven- and eight-year-olds. Embarrassed, he nonetheless studied hard and excelled as a student, apparently inspired by his pretty, red-haired teacher, Abigail Powers, whom he married seven years later.

At twenty-three Fillmore began clerking at a law firm and within four years was admitted to the bar. An avid bibliophile, he amassed a personal library of over four thousand volumes. He and his wife started the permanent White House library. Active in the civic affairs of his adopted home of Buffalo, he did not smoke, drink, or gamble. Instead, he founded civic institutions including the city's first high school, an adult self-improvement organization known as the Lyceum, the Young Men's Association, the Buffalo Mutual Fire Insurance Company, the Buffalo Fine Arts Academy, the Buffalo Historical Society, the University of Buffalo, and Buffalo General Hospital.

He served as a New York State assemblyman, U.S. congressman, New York State comptroller, and vice president, ascending to the presidency upon the death of President Zachary Taylor.

Fillmore's presidency was the first to be dominated by the issue of slavery. It affected all policy decisions, specifically which territories and states would be free and what laws would govern fugitive slaves in the North. Ten years prior to the outbreak of the Civil War, the occupant of the White House was busily forestalling a war between the states.

In 1852, Fillmore successfully dispatched Commodore Matthew C. Perry and four warships to Japan to open a port to United States trade.

Denied renomination, Fillmore retired from the presidency and went directly into mourning—his beloved Abigail had caught cold at the outdoor inaugural ceremonies of her husband's successor, Franklin Pierce, and within weeks died of pneumonia. Five years later, he married Caroline Carmichael McIntosh, the wealthy widow of a prominent Albany businessman.

Fillmore ran for president, unsuccessfully, one more time, in 1856, as the nominee of the American party. He died on March 8, 1874, after having suffered several strokes. His last words, as he accepted a spoonful of soup from his bedside doctor, were: "The nourishment is palatable."

☆ ☆ ☆

Where is the true-hearted American whose cheek does not tingle with shame to see our highest and most courted foreign missions filled by men of foreign birth to the exclusion of the native-born?

I believe that no one appointment has been made in this country that I had the honor to recommend . . . I regret it not. It has no power to grant what I have any desire to receive.

I need not say to you that I have no desire to run . . . I am not willing to be treacherously killed by this pretended kindness . . . Do not suppose for a moment that I think they desire my nomination.
(objecting to possible nomination for governor of New York)

Three years of civil war have desolated the fairest portion of our land; loaded the country with an enormous debt that the sweat of millions yet unborn must be taxed to pay; arrayed brother against brother, father against son in mortal combat; deluged our country with fraternal blood; whitened our battlefields with the bones of the slain; and darkened the sky with the pall of mourning.

The man who can look upon a crisis without being willing to offer himself upon the altar of his country is not fit for public trust.

I had not the advantage of a classical education, and no man should, in my judgment, accept a degree he cannot read.
(declining a degree from Oxford University)

I have no hostility to foreigners . . . Having witnessed their deplorable condition in the old country, God forbid I should add to their sufferings by refusing them an asylum in this.

It is a national disgrace that our Presidents, after having occupied the highest position in the country, should be cast adrift, and, perhaps, be compelled to keep a corner grocery for subsistence.

Let us remember that revolutions do not always establish freedom. Our own free institutions were not the offspring of our Revolution. They existed before.

An honorable defeat is better than a dishonorable victory.

☆ FRANKLIN PIERCE ☆

14th President

Birth: November 23, 1804   Death: October 8, 1869
Term: March 4, 1853–March 3, 1857

THE PIERCE PRESIDENCY

- *Kansas-Nebraska Act passed (permitted state residents to decide slavery issue, 1854)*
- *Gadsden Purchase from Mexico (for the land that makes up modern New Mexico and Arizona, 1853)*

Franklin Pierce's life ran fast—to college at age fifteen (where he hung out with Nathaniel Hawthorne and Henry Wadsworth Longfellow), New Hampshire state legislator at twenty-five, U.S. senator at thirty-two, elected (without running) to the presidency at forty-eight . . . and dumped by his political party at fifty-two.

Pierce came from a well-known New England family; his father served twice as governor of New Hampshire. A robust, active, and devilish youngster, he was quick to pick a fight or pull a prank. He attended Bowdoin College in Maine and eventually married the daughter, Jane Means Appleton, of that school's president. After college, Pierce studied law and was admitted to the bar in 1827.

He served in the New Hampshire Legislature, the U.S. House of Representatives, and the U.S. Senate. When the Democrats gathered in 1852 to nominate a presidential candidate, they could not agree to support any one of the four major candidates. After thirty-five ballots, Pierce's name—somewhat to his surprise—surfaced as a compromise choice. By the forty-ninth ballot, he was nominated, nearly unanimously.

Pierce's presidency was dominated by slavery issues, notably the bloody encounters between pro and antislavery forces in Kansas. Because he failed to maintain order in "Bleeding Kansas," he was deemed unelectable by members of his own Democratic party and was denied renomination in 1856. Instead the Democrats nominated James Buchanan.

During Pierce's term, the United States purchased, for $10 million, from Mexico, a 45,500-square-mile strip of land which today comprises southernmost Arizona and New Mexico. Pierce was also intent on extending the southern boundary of the United States by annexing Cuba, claiming, perhaps prophetically, "The Union can never enjoy repose, nor possess reliable security, as long as Cuba is not embraced within its boundaries." However, the *New York Herald* published sensitive details of the potential agreement (between the administration and Spain), which permanently halted negotiations.

Pierce's personal life was often touched by tragedy. His wife, petite, frail, shy, and melancholy, was a high-strung religious fanatic. She also always hated politics, and after all of their three sons died, the marriage disintegrated. At the White House, Jane wore black every day and spent much of her time writing notes to one of her dead sons. After she died in 1863, Pierce gave up his lifelong fight against alcoholism and drank heavily until his death in 1869 of "stomach inflammation."

☆ ☆ ☆

We Polked you in '44, We Shall Pierce you in '52.
(*campaign slogan*)

You have summoned me in my weakness. You must sustain me by your strength.
(inaugural address)

The stars upon your banner have become nearly threefold their original number; your densely populated possessions skirt the shores of the two great oceans.

So long as he [the American citizen] can discern every star in its place upon that ensign, without wealth to purchase for him preferment or title to purchase for him place, it will be his privilege, and must be his acknowledged right, to stand unabashed even in the presence of princes, with a proud consciousness that he is himself one of a nation of sovereigns.

No citizen of our country should permit himself to forget that he is a part of its Government and entitled to be heard in the determination of its policy and its measures, and that therefore the highest considerations of personal honor and patriotism require him to maintain by whatever power or influence he may possess the integrity of the laws of the Republic.

In a body where there are more than one hundred talking lawyers, you can make no calculation upon the termination of any debate and frequently, the more trifling the subject, the more animated and protracted the discussion.
(on Congress)

The storm of frenzy and faction must inevitably dash itself in vain against the unshaken rock of the Constitution.

The revenue of the country, levied almost insensibly to the taxpayer, goes on from year to year, increasing beyond either the interests or the prospective wants of the Government.

☆ JAMES BUCHANAN ☆

15th President

Birth: April 23, 1791   Death: June 1, 1868
Term: March 4, 1857–March 3, 1861

THE BUCHANAN PRESIDENCY

- *Confederate States of America organized (1861)*

- *Pony Express service begins (1860)*

- *Minnesota (1858), Oregon (1859), and Kansas (1861) admitted as states*

- *Southern states begin to secede from the Union (1860)*

The White House's only bachelor, Buchanan lived most of his life heartbroken. When twenty-eight, he was engaged; but following a lover's quarrel, his fiancée committed suicide. The experience scarred him permanently, and though he often enjoyed the company of beautiful women, he never married. His orphaned niece, Harriet Lane, whom he raised from childhood, served as official White House hostess during his administration.

Born in a log cabin in Cove Gap, Pennsylvania, Buchanan and his seven siblings moved to Mercersburg, where he attended the Old Stone Academy. Although he later studied hard at Dickinson College in Carlisle, he was also a troublemaker (at the end of his freshman year, the college urged his father to "keep his devilish son home"). In 1812, he was admitted to the Pennsylvania bar.

Buchanan served in the Third Cavalry during the War of 1812; he then served in the Pennsylvania House of Representatives, as a U.S. Representative, minister to Russia, U.S. senator, secretary of state, and minister to Great Britain. His depth and breadth of governmental and foreign-policy experience not only positioned him well for a run for the presidency, but his foreign service abroad had also kept him above the political fray surrounding the bitter and dividing issue of slavery. In 1856, he was unanimously nominated as a candidate for the presidency by the Democratic convention.

Buchanan was in office only two days, however, when the United States Supreme Court handed down its Dred Scott decision, which declared that Congress had no power to interfere with states' rights to regulate slavery. Northerners were furious and pledged to fight the decision, while southern states were threatening to secede from the Union. "You are sleeping on a volcano," Buchanan was warned. But he was unable to govern efficiently, torn between the belief that no state had a right to secede, but on the other hand, just as certain that the federal government had no legal right to stop a state from seceding.

By the time of the election of 1860, slavery was the one all-important issue. Buchanan's party failed to renominate him and the Republican candidate, Abraham Lincoln, was elected. During the several-month period between the election and Lincoln's taking office, one southern state after another left the Union. A lame duck, Buchanan was powerless, and in the end, quite pleased to hand over the office to Lincoln:

My dear sir, if you are as happy on entering the White House as I on leaving, you are a very happy man indeed.

After attending the inaugural of his successor, Buchanan returned to Lancaster, Pennsylvania. There he led a very private retirement, loyally supporting the Union and the Lincoln administration, and serving as a trustee for Franklin and Marshall College. Upon his death in 1868, he left an estate of over $300,000.

☆ ☆ ☆

Whatever the result may be, I shall carry to my grave the consciousness that I at least meant well for my country.

His disposition is as perverse and mulish as that of his father.
(on John Quincy Adams)

The distribution of patronage of the Government is by far the most disagreeable duty of the President. Applicants are so numerous, and their applications are pressed with such eagerness by their friends both in and out of Congress, that the selection of one for any desirable office gives offense to many.

Liberty must be allowed to work out its natural results; and these will, ere long, astonish the world.

From Caesar to Cromwell, and from Cromwell to Napoleon . . . history presents the same solemn warning—beware of elevating to the highest civil trust the commander of our victorious armies.

Capital and capitalists . . . Are proverbially timid.

If those forts [in Charleston] should be taken by South Carolina in consequence of our neglect to put them in defensible condition, it were better for you and me both to be thrown into the Potomac with millstones tied about our necks.
(to Secretary of War John B. Floyd, 1860)

Abstract propositions should never be discussed by a legislative body.

[Constitutions are] restraints imposed, not by arbitrary authority, but by people upon themselves and their own representatives.

There is nothing stable but Heaven and the Constitution.

The ballot box is the surest arbiter of disputes among freemen.

It is better to bear the ills we have than to fly to others we know not of.

What, sir! Prevent the American people from crossing the Rocky Mountains? You might as well command Niagara not to flow. We must fulfill our destiny.

Restraint, restraint . . . this Federal Government is nothing but a system of restraints from beginning to end.

We have met the enemy and we are theirs.
(*on losing an election*)

It is beyond question the destiny of our race to spread themselves over the continent of North America . . . The tide of emigrants will flow to the South.

What is right and what is practicable are two different things.

☆ ABRAHAM LINCOLN ☆

16th President

Birth: February 12, 1809   Death: April 15, 1865
Term: March 4, 1861–April 15, 1865

THE LINCOLN PRESIDENCY

- *Civil War (1861–65)*
- *Emancipation Proclamation issued (1863)*
- *West Virginia (1863) and Nevada (1864) admitted as states*

Lincoln, who was deeply interested in psychic phenomena, participated in several séances at the White House, including one in which a piano was raised and moved around the room. It was the professional opinion of the mediums who worked with him that he was definitely possessed of extraordinary psychic powers. A week before his assassination, he dreamed that he was walking about the White House, in search of the sound of sobbing. When he came to the East Room, he saw a coffin draped in black. "Who is dead?" Lincoln asked. "The president," he was told. And on the very day of his assassination, Lincoln told his Cabinet that he had seen himself sailing "in an indescribable vessel and moving rapidly toward an indistinct shore."

Lincoln was born in a dirt-floor log cabin, into a poor Kentucky family headed by a father who never learned to read or write. Lincoln's mother died when he was ten, soon after the family had moved to Indiana. His father married again, to Sarah Johnston, who brought warmth and encouragement to the family, and who Lincoln called his "best friend in this world."

Lincoln had little schooling, yet he loved to read, dipping into the family Bible and borrowing books whenever he could. "My best friend," he once said, "is the man who'll git me a book I ain't read."

When he was twenty-one, the Lincolns moved again, to Illinois. A year later, Abe left home, settled in New Salem, Illinois, and worked as a general-store clerk. In 1832, he joined the military to serve in the Black Hawk War. Little happened, as he readily admitted, joking that the only blood "I lost in defense of my country was to mosquitoes."

He failed as a partner in a general store before securing the position of postmaster of New Salem. He then served in the Illinois Legislature but failed to win a second term. With his public career apparently ended, he returned to Illinois to practice law. But the question of slavery was being debated with even more fury throughout the country, and Lincoln's strong and articulate antislavery position was well known: "New free states are places for poor people to go and better their condition; they should not be turned over to rich slave owners." In 1858, Lincoln ran for the U.S. Senate against Stephen A. Douglas, and in a famous series of speeches, Lincoln and Douglas debated the issue of slavery in the new states. Douglas won the election, but the debates made Lincoln famous. Soon thereafter, he was asked by the Republicans to be their presidential candidate in 1860.

Lincoln had married Mary Todd in 1842. Although she possessed a ready wit and a sparkling personality, she was mentally unstable and suffered from agonizing migraine headaches. In the White House where she was charged by political enemies with being a Confederate sympathizer, she became paranoid and irrationally jealous of those around the president. She responded by going on spending sprees (one such spree totaled $27,000—including the purchase of 300 pairs of gloves within 120 days). She and Lincoln lost a son, Willie, in 1862; then she lost Lincoln in 1864; and another son, Tad, in 1871. Finally, in 1875, her one surviving son, Robert, had her committed to a mental institution.

After her release and prior to her death in 1882, she traveled quite a bit, including a tour of Europe.

After winning against Douglas in the bitter election of 1860, Lincoln took office in March 1861. In April, southern soldiers fired on the Union-held Fort Sumter in Charleston, South Carolina. The Civil War had begun.

The next four years were probably the most desperate in the history of the United States. Lincoln proved himself to be a great president. He dedicated his efforts to saving the Union, which to his mind was not just a collection of states but the most important democratic government in the world—*ever*.

He succeeded in spite of mediocre military leaders, wavering political support, and a very spirited and dedicated southern cause. By the fall of 1864 it was obvious that the North would win the war, and Lincoln prepared for when the crippled Union would again be one nation. Revenge against the South would not do, he warned: "Blood cannot restore blood, and government should not act for revenge."

Reelected in 1864, he spoke of a vision:

With malice toward none, with charity for all, with firmness in the right, as God gives us to see the right, let us strive on to finish the work we are in, to bind up the nation's wounds, to care for him who shall have borne the battle, and for his widow and his orphan—to do all which may achieve and cherish a just and lasting peace among ourselves and with all nations.

The dream was not to be. Weeks after these words were spoken, and just days after the final surrender of Robert E. Lee to Ulysses S. Grant, Lincoln was assassinated. One of the greatest men in all American history lay dead. He lay in state in fourteen cities over a two-and-a-half-week period before being buried in Springfield, his decomposed face blackened and withered.

☆ ☆ ☆

No one, not in my situation can appreciate my feeling of sadness at this parting. To this place, and the kindness of these people, I owe everything. Here I have lived a quarter of a century, and have passed from a young to an old man. Here my children have been born, and one is buried. I now leave, not knowing when or whether ever I may return, with a task before me greater than that which rested upon Washington. Without the assistance of that Divine Being who ever attended him, I cannot succeed. With that assistance I cannot fail. Trusting in Him who can go with me, and remain with you, and be everywhere for good, let us confidently hope that all will yet be well.
(*farewell address, Springfield, Illinois, February 11, 1861*)

The legitimate object of government is to do for a community of people whatever they need to have done, but cannot do at all in their separate and individual capacities.

Among free men there can be no successful appeal from the ballot to the bullet; and those who take such appeal are sure to lose their cause and pay the costs.

As I would not be a slave, so I would not be a master. This expresses my idea of democracy. Whatever differs from this, to the extent of the difference, is no democracy.

As a nation, we began by declaring that "all men are created equal." We now practically read it, "All men are created equal, except Negroes." When the Know-Nothings get control, it will read, "All men are created equal, except Negroes, and foreigners, and Catholics." When it comes to this I should prefer emigrating to some other country where they make no pretense of loving liberty—to Russia, for instance, where despotism can be taken pure, without the base alloy of hypocrisy.

I think the authors of that notable instrument [the Declaration of Independence] intended to include all men, but they did not intend to declare all men equal in all respects. The did not mean to say all men were equal in color, size, intellect, moral developments, or social capacity. They defined with tolerable distinctness in what respects they did consider all men created equal—equal with "certain unalienable rights, among which are life, liberty, and the pursuit of happiness."

The *probability* that we may fall in the struggle *ought not* to deter us from the support of a cause we believe to be just; it *shall not* deter me.

If slavery is not wrong, nothing is wrong.

To sin by silence when they should protest makes cowards of men.

Men moving only in an official circle are apt to become merely official—not to say arbitrary—in their ideas, and are apter and apter with each passing day to forget that they only hold power in a representative capacity.

A nation may be said to consist of its territory, its people, and its laws. The territory is the only part which is of certain durability. Laws change, people die; the land remains.

A fellow once came to me to ask for an appointment as a minister abroad. Finding he could not get that, he came down to some more modest position. Finally he asked to be made a tide-waiter. When he saw he could not get that, he asked me for an old pair of trousers. It is sometimes well to be humble.

But, if this country cannot be saved without giving up that principle [equality] . . . I would rather be assassinated on this spot than surrender it.

If it [the Ship of State] should suffer attack now, there will be no pilot ever needed for another voyage.

When the hour comes for dealing with slavery, I trust I will be willing to do my duty though it cost my life.

I pray that our Heavenly Father may assuage the anguish of your bereavement, and leave you only the cherished memory of the loved and lost, and the solemn pride that must be yours to have laid so costly a sacrifice upon the altar of freedom.
(From a letter to a Mrs. Bixby, who, Lincoln was told, had lost five sons in battle. It was later discovered that two were lost.)

Let us have faith that right makes might, and in that faith let us to the end dare to do our duty as we understand it.

If it is [God's] will that I must die at the hand of an assassin, I must be resigned. I must do my duty as I see it, and leave the rest with God.
(1864)

My dear McClellan [Major General George B.]: If you don't want to use the Army I should like to borrow it for a while.
(to his overly cautious major general, 1862)

To correct evils, great and small, which spring from want of sympathy and from positive enmity among strangers, as nations or as individuals, is one of the highest functions of civilizations.

What is conservatism? Is it not adherence to the old and tried, against the new and untried?

I wish some of you would tell me the brand of whiskey that Grant drinks. I would like to send a barrel of it to my other generals.

I have endured a great deal of ridicule without much malice, and have received a great deal of kindness, not quite free from ridicule. I am used to it.

It has long been a grave question whether any government, not too strong for the liberties of its people, can be strong enough to maintain its existence in emergencies.

I may not have made as great a President as some other man, but I believe I have kept these discordant elements together as well as anyone could.

Truth is generally the best vindication against slander.

I desire so to conduct the affairs of this administration that if at the end, when I come to lay down the reins of power, I have lost every other friend on earth, I shall at least have one friend left, and that friend shall be down inside me.

Having thus chosen our course, without guile and with pure purpose, let us renew our trust in God, and go forward without fear and with manly hearts.
(message to Congress, July 4, 1861)

These capitalists generally act harmoniously and in concert, to fleece the people.

The dogmas of the quiet past are inadequate to the stormy present. The occasion is piled high with difficulty, and we must rise with the occasion. As our case is new, so we must think anew and act anew.

Character is like a tree and reputation like its shadow. The shadow is what we think of it; the tree is the real thing.

God must have loved the plain people; he made so many of them.

He can compress the most words into the smallest ideas of any man I ever met.

It has been my experience that folks who have no vices have very few virtues.

Whenever I hear anyone arguing for slavery, I feel a strong impulse to see it tried on him personally.

Books serve to show a man that those original thoughts of his aren't very new after all.

With malice toward none, with charity for all, with firmness in the right as God gives us to see the right, let us strive on to finish the work we are in, to bind up the nation's wounds, to care for him who shall have borne the battle, and for his widow and his orphan, to do all which may achieve and cherish a just and lasting peace among ourselves, and with all nations. . . .

It is now for them [the American people] to demonstrate to the world that those who can fairly carry an election can also suppress a rebellion; that ballots are the rightful and peaceful successors of bullets, and that when ballots have fairly and constitutionally decided, there can be no successful appeal back to bullets. . . . Such will be a great lesson of peace: teaching men that what they cannot take by an election, neither can they take it by war.

The ballot is stronger than the bullet.

Prohibition will work great injury to the cause of temperance. It is a species of intemperance within itself, for it goes beyond the bounds of reason in that it attempts to control a man's appetite by legislation, and makes a crime out of things that are not crimes. A Prohibition law strikes a blow at the very principles upon which our government was founded.

I claim not to have controlled events, but confess plainly that events have controlled me.

If I were to try to read, much less answer, all the attacks made on me, this shop might as well be closed for any other business. I do the very best I know how—the very best I can; and I mean to keep doing so until the end. If the end brings me out wrong, ten angels swearing I was right would make no difference.

I hate [slavery] because it deprives the republican example of its just influence in the world—enables the enemies of free institutions, with plausibility, to taunt us as hypocrites—causes the real friends of freedom to doubt our sincerity.

"A house divided against itself cannot stand." I believe this government cannot endure permanently half slave and half free. I do not expect the Union to be dissolved—I do not expect the house to fall—but I do expect it will cease to be divided. It will become all one thing, or all the other.

If you once forfeit the confidence of your fellow citizens, you can never regain their respect and esteem. It is true that you may fool all the people some of the time; you can even fool some of the people all the time; but you can't fool all of the people all the time.

Fourscore and seven years ago our fathers brought forth on this continent, a new nation, conceived in Liberty, and dedicated to the proposition that all men are created equal.

Important principles may and must be inflexible.

Whatever woman may cast her lot with mine, should any ever do so, it is my intention to do all in my power to make her happy and contented; and there is nothing I can imagine that would make me more unhappy than to fail in the effort.

I do not allow myself to suppose that either the convention or the League have concluded to decide that I am either the greatest or the best man in America, but rather they have concluded that it is not best to swap horses while crossing the river, and have further concluded that I am not so poor a horse that they might not make a botch of it in trying to swap.
(*on his renomination as president, 1864*)

Tact is the ability to describe others as they see themselves.

But, in a larger sense, we cannot dedicate—we cannot consecrate—we cannot hallow—this ground. The brave men, living and dead, who struggled here, have consecrated it far above our poor power to add or detract. The world will little note nor long remember what we say here, but it can never forget what they did here. It is for us, the living, rather to be dedicated here to the unfinished work which they who fought here have thus far so nobly advanced. It is rather for us to be here dedicated to the great task

remaining before us—that from these honored dead we take increased devotion to that cause for which they gave the last full measure of devotion; that we here highly resolve that these dead shall not have died in vain; that this nation, under God, shall have a new birth of freedom; and that government of the people, by the people, for the people, shall not perish from the earth.
(address at Gettysburg, 1863)

☆ ANDREW JOHNSON ☆

17th President

Birth: December 29, 1808   Death: July 31, 1875
Term: April 15, 1865–March 3, 1869

THE JOHNSON (ANDREW) PRESIDENCY

- *Thirteenth Amendment (abolishing slavery, 1865) and Fourteenth Amendment (establishing rights of citizens, 1868) to the Constitution ratified*
- *Nebraska (1867) admitted as a state*
- *Alaska purchased from Russia (1867)*

Born into a poor, hardworking North Carolina family, young Andrew Johnson never had the money or opportunity for schooling. Instead, he learned to be a tailor, eventually setting up a business in Tennessee. Throughout his successful political career, he continued to make his own clothes, taking such pride in his skills that while governor of Tennessee, he complimented the governor of Kentucky by making a suit for him.

Johnson eventually learned to read and write by painstakingly teaching himself and later, with assistance from his wife, Eliza McCardle. She (age sixteen) and Johnson (age eighteen) wed in 1827. She patiently tutored her husband, also teaching him math and improving his spelling. While he labored in the tailor shop, she often read aloud to him. Sadly, however, by the time the Johnsons took up residency in the White House, her health was failing. Too ill to preside as First Lady, she made only two public appearances in the nearly four years of the Johnson presidency; her daughter, Mrs. Martha Patter, handled official White House social duties.

Johnson began his political career as an alderman, then mayor, of Greeneville, Tennessee. He served in the Tennessee House of Representatives, in the Tennessee Senate, in the U.S. Congress, as governor of Tennessee, and in the U.S. Senate. After Lincoln's election, the southern states—including Tennessee—left the Union. As the states seceded, every southerner left Congress except Johnson: "I voted against Lincoln. I spoke against him. I spent my money to defeat him. But still I love my country."

This made Johnson something of a hero in the North so that when Lincoln ran for a second term, Vice President Hannibal Hamlin was dumped from the ticket and the Republicans instead nominated Johnson. Upon ascending to the presidency, Johnson sought to carry out the lenient Reconstruction of the South envisioned by Lincoln. However he did not have Lincoln's generous skills of persuasion and leadership, qualities desperately needed in the turbulent years that followed such a bitter internal war. Many politicians pursued profit and opportunity, disrupting Johnson's intentions. Eventually, he began to remove some of these "Radical Republicans" from office, including those in his own Cabinet who were undermining his policies.

This angered many northern politicians and for the first time in the nation's history, Congress moved to impeach a president. After only a one-vote margin in Congress kept Johnson in office, his chances of reelection seemed slim.

He returned to Tennessee, where six years later he was again elected to the U.S. Senate. Upon returning to the Capitol, he was warmly greeted by the same politicians who only years earlier had attempted to remove him from office.

Johnson died on July 31, 1875, a belated victim of the deadly cholera epidemic of 1873. Among his last writings were these thoughts:

I have performed my duty to my God, my country, and my family. I have nothing to fear in approaching death. To me it is the mere shadow of God's protecting wing. . . . Here I will rest in quiet and peace beyond the reach of calumny's poisoned shaft, the influence of envy and jealous enemies, where treason and traitors or State backsliders and hypocrites in church can have no peace.

Of all the dangers which our nation has yet encountered, none are equal to those which must result from success of the current effort to Africanize the southern half of the country.
(on proposals to grant blacks the right to vote)

I have been informed that part of the business to be transacted on the present occasion is the assassination of the individual who now has the honor of addressing you. . . . Therefore, if any man has come here tonight for the purpose indicated, I do not say to him, let him speak, but, let him shoot.
(1855, when campaigning for governor of Tennessee in an area that was a stronghold of his opponents)

The goal to strive for is a poor government but a rich people.

If I am shot at, I want no man to be in the way of the bullet.
(rejecting bodyguards after an assassination threat)

I have been almost overwhelmed by the announcement of the sad event [Lincoln's assassination] which has so recently occurred. I feel incompetent to perform duties so important and responsible as those which have been so unexpectedly thrown upon me.

I hold it the duty of the Executive to insist upon frugality in the expenditure, and a sparing economy is itself a great national resource.

Honest conviction is my courage; the Constitution is my guide.

Notwithstanding a mendacious press; notwithstanding a subsidized gang of hirelings who have not ceased to traduce me, I have discharged all my official duties and fulfilled my pledges. And I say here tonight that if my predecessor [Lincoln] had lived, the vials of wrath would have poured out upon him.

Outside of the Constitution we have no legal authority more than private citizens, and within it we have only so much as that instrument gives us. This broad principle limits all our functions and applies to all subjects.

Slavery exists. It is black in the South, and white in the North.

A railroad! It would frighten horses, put the owners of public vehicles out of business, break up inns and taverns, and be a monopoly generally.

☆ Ulysses Simpson Grant ☆

18th President

Birth: April 27, 1822   Death: July 23, 1885
Term: March 4, 1869–March 3, 1877

THE GRANT PRESIDENCY

• *First transcontinental railroad service (1869)*

• *Colorado admitted as a state (1876)*

• *General George Armstrong Custer's troops destroyed at Little Bighorn (1876)*

Ironically, this hard-drinking man's man who achieved fame on the battlefield was particularly squeamish at the sight of animal blood. As an otherwise hardworking child, Grant avoided work in his father's tannery where the blood-caked hides nauseated him. If he ate meat at all, it had to be cooked black, and he never ate poultry. "I could never eat anything," he explained, "that went on two legs." For breakfast, he most often ate a cucumber soaked in vinegar.

Although Grant was born in Point Pleasant, Ohio (just north of Cincinnati), while he was still an infant his family moved to Georgetown, Ohio, where he was raised. A decent student, he hoped to be either a farmer or to work the rivers as a trader. However, his father, without Grant's knowledge, arranged for his appointment to West Point. Although he excelled in horsemanship (as he had since early childhood), his career at the U.S. Military Academy was mediocre at best.

Grant married Julia Boggs Dent in 1848. They were devoted both to each other and to their children. Mrs. Grant entertained lavishly as First Lady and Grant's favorite child, Nellie, a celebrated beauty, was married at age seventeen in a spectacular White House wedding.

After his graduation from West Point, Grant served in the Mexican War (1846–48)—albeit reluctantly—for he believed the United States to be the aggressor:

> I have never altogether forgiven myself for going into that . . . I do not think there was ever a more wicked war than that waged by the United States on Mexico. I thought so at the time, when I was a youngster, only I had not moral courage enough to resign.

Grant left the military in 1854, at a time when he was drinking heavily, and unsuccessfully pursued a series of jobs including farming, selling wood, real estate, civil service, and at last, in 1860, clerking at his father's leather goods store.

With the outbreak of the Civil War in 1861, Grant resumed his military career as a colonel, posting one victory after another, working his way up through the ranks to general. He made full use of his numerical advantage (in soldiers) over the South, with his own casualties often being very high. None of his victories was especially ingenious or spectacular, but all were effective and forceful. In February 1862, upon capturing Fort Donelson, Tennessee, Grant uttered his famous ultimatum to Confederate General Simon B. Buckner: "No terms except an unconditional and immediate surrender can be accepted." This earned him the nickname Unconditional Surrender Grant.

When Robert E. Lee's forces finally surrendered in 1865, Grant was magnanimous, exacting lenient terms of surrender. Confederate officers were permitted to return home with their sidearms, mounted forces could keep their horses for plowing, and all were treated with dignity.

A national war hero, Grant had no serious opposition for the Republican presidential nomination in 1868, and he won the general election just as easily, quietly running on the simple theme of "Let us have peace." After four years of war and three years of bitter Reconstruction, the public embraced the promise.

Outside the army Grant proved to be a very poor judge of men. He appointed friends and relatives to high positions in the government where they cheated, stole, and took bribes. Although rigidly incorruptible himself, Grant saw his presidency marked by several major scandals—some reaching as high as his Cabinet and as close as his brother-in-law. Nonetheless, he was easily reelected to a second term. Although his personal popularity endured, the corruption continued throughout his second term.

Upon retirement from the White House, Grant and his family went on a world tour, traveling through Europe, Asia, and Africa. Returning home and seemingly not yet having learned the danger of trusting "friends," Grant invested all his money plus borrowed funds in a banking firm. It soon went belly-up and Grant was left with huge debts. Beginning in the fall of 1884, he raced against terminal throat cancer (he had smoked twenty cigars a day throughout much of his life) to complete his memoirs so that they might provide his widow with financial security. They did. These memoirs, the last words of which he wrote just three days before his death in July, 1885, were a major best-seller.

☆ ☆ ☆

The art of war is simple enough. Find out where your enemy is. Get at him as soon as you can. Strike at him as hard as you can, and keep moving on.

I am more of a farmer than a soldier. I take little or no interest in military affairs.
(1879)

[There is] but one debt contracted in the last four years which the people of the United States cannot pay. That is the debt of gratitude to the rank and file of our Army and Navy.

It [campaigning] has been done, so far as I remember, by but two presidential candidates heretofore, and both of them were public speakers and both were beaten. I am no speaker and I don't want to be beaten.

A measure which makes at once 4,000,000 people voters who were heretofore declared by the highest tribunal in the land not citizens of the United States, not eligible to become so . . . is indeed a measure of grander importance than any other act of the kind from the foundation of our free Government to the present day.
(on the Thirteenth Amendment, the abolishment of slavery)

Social equality is not a subject to be legislated upon.

Our Union rests upon public opinion, and can never be cemented by the blood of its citizens shed in civil war.

When news of the [Lee's] surrender first reached our lines our men commenced firing a salute of a hundred guns in honor of the victory. I at once sent word, however, to have it stopped. The Confederates were now our prisoners, and we did not want to exult over their downfall.

Leave the matter of religion to the family altar, the church, and the private school, supported entirely by private contributions. Keep the church and the State forever separate.

Labor disgraces no man; unfortunately you occasionally find men disgrace labor.

I know no method to secure the repeal of bad or obnoxious laws so effective as their stringent execution.

I shall on all subjects have a policy to recommend, but none to enforce against the will of the people.

I would suggest the taxation of all property equally whether church or corporation.

There never was a time when, in my opinion, some way could not be found to prevent the drawing of the sword.

The right of revolution is an inherent one. When people are oppressed by their government, it is a natural right they enjoy to relieve themselves of the oppression, if they are strong enough, either by withdrawal from it, or by overthrowing it and substituting a government more acceptable.

My failures have been errors of judgment, not of intent.

God gave us Lincoln and Liberty; let us fight for both.

I felt like anything rather than rejoicing at the downfall of a foe who had fought so long and so valiantly.
(on the surrender of Lee)

RUTHERFORD
☆ BIRCHARD HAYES ☆

19th President

Birth: October 4, 1822   Death: January 17, 1893
Term: March 4, 1877–March 3, 1881

THE HAYES PRESIDENCY

- *Last federal troops pulled from the South, ending Reconstruction (1877)*
- *New York City becomes first United States city with a population of one million (1880)*
- *Intent to construct the Panama Canal announced (1880)*

Although well educated and highly respected, Rutherford B. Hayes was not one of our more exciting presidents. The First Lady, Lucy Hayes, banned all alcoholic beverages from the White House and became known as "Lemonade Lucy." And the very favorite presidential diversion was Sunday-night hymn singing.

Hayes was born in 1822, eleven weeks after his father's death. Raised by his mother and his maternal uncle, a bachelor, Hayes proved to be an industrious, informed, polite, and respectful student. He graduated from Kenyon College as class valedictorian in 1842 and was admitted to the Ohio bar in 1845, two months after graduation from Harvard Law School. Two years later he met Lucy Ware Webb, whom he married in 1852. A graduate of Wesleyan Women's College in Cincinnati, she was the first First Lady with a college degree.

Hayes then served as Cincinnati City Solicitor, U.S. congressman, and governor of Ohio. During the Civil War he rose from major to major general, took part in over fifty engagements, was wounded several times—once seriously, and on four occasions, his horse was shot out from under him.

Nominated for the presidency by the Republicans in 1876, Hayes ran 250,000 votes behind Democrat Samuel Tilden, but the count in the Electoral College was disputed. In the most controversial electoral decision in American history, Hayes was awarded all the 19 contested electors at the last minute—giving him a razor-thin 185–184 "victory." Despite having his apparent victory at the polls negated by an electoral commission voting strictly along party lines, a resigned Tilden put the best light on the situation: "I can retire to private life with the consciousness that I shall receive from posterity the credit of having been elected to the highest position in the gift of the people, without any of the cares and responsibilities of the office."

Although his election could hardly be described as a mandate or even a strong endorsement, Hayes soon came to be respected as an honest, hardworking, and serious-minded president. He made great efforts to restore integrity to the White House after Grant's scandalous administration, reforming the civil service and issuing an executive order barring federal employees from taking part in political activities. As Hayes had promised throughout the election, he withdrew the last federal troops from the South, thus ending Reconstruction and effectively restoring white supremacy to that region. He also faced the initial wave of immigration, as the first of more than eleven million people from abroad who would arrive over the next thirty years began to pour into the United States. For the first time, Chinese immigration into California was restricted.

Having renounced a second term upon acceptance of the Republican nomination four years earlier, Hayes happily retired into an active life dedicated to prison reform, education, and support for specific political candidates and issues. His wife, Lucy, died of a stroke in 1889. Hayes, after having suffered a series of heart attacks, died on January 17, 1893, in the arms of his son, Webb. His last words were: "I know that I am going where Lucy is."

☆ ☆ ☆

Nobody ever left the presidency with less regret, less disappointment, fewer heartburnings, or any general content with the result of his term (in his own heart, I mean) than I do.

All appointments hurt. Five friends are made cold or hostile for every appointment; no new friends are made. All patronage is perilous to men of real ability or merit. It aids only those who lack other claims to public support.

The President of the United States of necessity owes his election to office to the suffrage and zealous labors of a political party the members of which cherish with ardor and regard as of essential importance the principles of their party organization; but he should strive to be always mindful of the fact that he serves his party best who serves his country best.

I feel that defeat will be a great relief—a setting free from bondage.
(regarding his nomination as the Republican candidate for president)

Let me assure my countrymen of the Southern States that it is my earnest desire to regard and promote their truest interest—the interests of the white and of the colored people both and equally—and to put forth my best efforts in behalf of a civil policy which will forever wipe out in our political affairs the color line and the distinction between North and South, to the end that we may have not merely a united North or a united South, but a united country.

Nothing like it ever before in the Executive Mansion—liquor, snobbery, and worse.
(on Chester A. Arthur's White House)

Abolish plutocracy if you would abolish poverty.

Let all our dealings with the Red man be characterized by justice and good faith, and let there be the most liberal provision for his physical wants, for education in its widest sense, and for religious instruction and training.

In politics I am growing indifferent. I would like it, if I could now return to my planting and books at home.
(1876)

My policy is trust—peace, and to put aside the bayonet.

Sectionalism and race prejudice . . . are the only two enemies America has any cause to fear.

Well I am heartily tired of this life of bondage, responsibility and toil.
(on the presidency)

Only a few Presidents have had the felicity to see their party stronger at the close of their terms than it was at the beginning. Only a few have left their country more prosperous than they found it.

Let me emphasize in my last message the idea that the Constitution should be so amended as to lengthen the term of the President to six years, and so as to render him ineligible for a second term.

I would honor the man who would give to his country a good newspaper.

It is now true that this is God's Country, if equal rights—a fair start and an equal chance in the race of life are everywhere secured to all.

The melancholy thing in our public life is the insane desire to get higher.

☆ James Abram Garfield ☆

20th President

Birth: November 19, 1831   Death: September 19, 1881
Term: March 4, 1881–September 19, 1881

THE GARFIELD PRESIDENCY

- *American Red Cross founded (1881)*
- *Garfield dies two and a half months after having been shot (1881)*

James A. Garfield—the last president to be born in a log cabin, the first to be left-handed, and the second to die from an assassin's bullet—had a premonition of his own death. Just two days before he was shot, he even sent for Robert Lincoln, son of the late president, and asked him to recount his memories of his father's assassination.

Garfield was born in 1831 in Orange, Ohio; his family found itself in extreme poverty only two years later when his father died. As a child he read voraciously, especially American history and sea adventures. At sixteen, over his mother's strong objections, he sought to fulfill his childhood dream of becoming a sailor. However, he got no further than being a "tow boy," driving the horses and mules that pulled the boats on the Ohio Canal. He soon turned with more seriousness to his studies, eventually entering Williams College (Williamstown, Massachusetts) where he blossomed intellectually while supporting himself as a janitor. A speech by Ralph Waldo Emerson greatly impressed him, prodding him to a life of study and self-improvement. After graduating first in his class, he found employment as a professor of classics (one of his favorite tricks was simultaneously to write Latin with one hand and Greek with the other). But campus life lacked sufficient stimulation; so Garfield took up the study of law on his own for two years until he was admitted to the Ohio bar in 1860.

When the Civil War broke out, Garfield raised a regiment of volunteer soldiers, many of whom were his former students. Lacking any military training, he turned again to his study skills, reading everything he could on military tactics. It worked. Garfield became so excellent an officer that at age thirty-one he was made the youngest brigadier general in the army.

He served as an Ohio state senator and a U.S. representative. He was a compromise candidate for the presidency, nominated by the Republicans on the thirty-sixth convention ballot. Chester A. Arthur was then nominated as vice president to placate those Republicans who had not supported Garfield.

In pre–Civil Service times, when *every* government job was handed out to friends and political supporters, office seekers would swarm to the White House after the inauguration. Among them in 1881 was a mentally unstable Garfield supporter, Charles J. Guiteau, who intended to land a diplomatic position. When Guiteau was firmly rebuffed, he plotted to assassinate Garfield. He even specifically purchased a .44 British Bulldog, an expensive pistol, because he thought it would look attractive in a museum. After stalking the president for three weeks, Guiteau finally shot Garfield, seriously wounding him, on July 1, 1881, less than four months after his presidency had begun.

Eighty days later, Garfield died; and Guiteau wrote to the new president, Chester A. Arthur:

My inspiration is a Godsend to you and I presume that you appreciate it . . . It raised you from a political cypher to the president of the United States.

The assassin's letter then goes on to offer much counsel, including advice on the selection of his new Cabinet. Almost a year later, on June 30, 1882, Guiteau was hanged.

☆ ☆ ☆

All free governments are managed by the combined wisdom and folly of the people.

My God! What is there in this place that a man should ever want to get into it?
(on the presidency)

Talleyrand once said to the first Napoleon that "the United States is a giant without bones." Since that time our gristle has been rapidly hardening.

The spirit of that clause of the Constitution which shields them [members of Congress] from arrest "during their attendance on the session of their respective houses, and in going to and from the same," should also shield them from being arrested from their legislative work, morning, noon, and night, by office-seekers.

My day is frittered away by personal seeking of people, when it ought to be given to the great problem[s] which concern the whole country. Four years of this kind of intellectual dissipation may cripple me for the remainder of my life. What might not a vigorous thinker do, if he could be allowed to use the opportunities of a presidential term in vital, useful activity! Some Civil Service reform will come by necessity after the wearisome years of wasted Presidents have paved the way for it.

[The President is] the last person in the world to know what the people really want and think.

They open their mouths for a horse, but are perfectly willing to settle for a fly.
(on office seekers)

I spoke almost every day till the election, but it now appears that we are defeated by the combined power of rebellion, Catholicism and whiskey, a trinity very hard to conquer.
(on attempts to unite the Republican party for the election of 1880)

We may divide the whole struggle of the human race into two chapters: first, the fight to get leisure; and then the second fight of civilization—what shall we do with our leisure when we get it.

Whoever controls the volume of money in any country is absolute master of all industry and commerce.

I am an advocate of paper money, but that paper money must represent what it professes on its face. I do not wish to hold in my hands the printed lies of the government.

For mere vengeance I would do nothing. This nation is too great to look for mere revenge. But for the security of the future I would do everything.
(on the assassination of Lincoln)

The real political issues of the day declare themselves, and come out of the depths of that deep which we call public opinion.

A nation is not worthy to be saved if, in the hour of its fate, it will not gather up all its jewels of manhood and life, and go down into the conflict, however bloody and doubtful, resolved on measureless ruin or complete success.

A pound of pluck is worth a ton of luck.

There is nothing . . . so inspiring as the possibilities that lie locked up in the head and breast of a young man.

Justice and goodwill will outlast passion.

We shall never know why slavery dies so hard in this Republic . . . till we know why Sin is long-lived and Satan is immortal.

I love agitation and investigation and glory in defending unpopular truth against popular error.

I have had many troubles in my life, but the worst of them never came.

I am receiving what I suppose to be the usual number of threatening letters on that subject. Assassination can be not more guarded against than death by lightning; and it is best not to worry about either.

My God! What is this! Assassination . . .
(*overheard by Secretary of State James Blaine at the time of Garfield's assassination*)

He must have been crazy. None but an insane person could have done such a thing. What could he have wanted to shoot me for?
(*on his deathbed*)

☆ CHESTER ALAN ARTHUR ☆

21st President

Birth: October 5, 1830   Death: November 18, 1886
Term: September 20, 1881–March 3, 1885

THE ARTHUR PRESIDENCY

• *Pendleton Act creates Civil Service System (1883)*

• *Washington monument dedicated (1885)*

A high-living, elegantly dressed, fashionable, and wealthy wine connoisseur with a French cook (he usually spent two to three hours at the dinner table), Chester A. Arthur refused to live among the hodgepodge of furniture in the White House. Not until twenty-four full wagon loads of furnishings (some of it priceless) were auctioned off and the entire White House redone in late-Victorian style would "Elegant Arthur" (as he was nicknamed) even consider sleeping there.

Named after the doctor who delivered him (Dr. Chester Abell), Arthur was born in North Fairfield, Vermont (although political opponents, in an effort to disqualify Arthur constitutionally from the presidency, often charged that he was born across the border, in Canada). Arthur's father, a Baptist minister, was frequently transferred from parish to parish, so that the future president grew up in the Vermont towns of North Fairfield, Williston, and Hinesburg and the New York communities of Perry, York, Union Village (now Greenwich), Schenectady, and Hoosick.

Arthur attended Union College, where he was known to engage in campus pranks such as dumping the school bell into the Erie

Canal. Eventually he took up the study of law and was admitted to the New York bar in 1854.

At the age of thirty, he married Ellen "Nell" Lewis Herndon, twenty-two. Although it was apparently a strong marriage, it suffered the strains of Arthur's many political activities and his military service. In 1880, Mrs. Arthur suddenly developed pneumonia and died within two days. Away on business at the time, Arthur arrived home too late to see his wife conscious again. He was inconsolable and never fully recovered from her death, regretful that she never lived to become First Lady. As president, Arthur ordered fresh flowers placed daily before her portrait in the White House.

Arthur's administrative skills were clearly evident during his military service. From February 1858 to December 1862, Arthur served in the New York State militia, rising from brigade judge advocate to quartermaster general. Said Governor Edwin D. Morgan, "Arthur was my chief reliance in the duties of equipping and transporting troops and munitions of war. . . . he displayed not only great executive ability and unbending integrity, but great knowledge of Army Regulations. He can say No (which is important) without giving offense."

Arthur's early law practice was active in the antislavery movement. As a junior partner in the firm of Culver, Parker, and Arthur, he took on many cases with the hope of testing the constitutionality of those laws that supported the practice of slavery. He served as Collector of the Port of New York prior to being nominated as the Republican vice presidential candidate (an effort to placate those conservative Republicans whose candidate, former President Ulysses S. Grant, had lost the presidential nomination to James Garfield).

Only months after Arthur became vice president, President Garfield was shot by a frustrated office seeker. Arthur's political cronies were jubilant at the news. They expected Arthur—himself a product and long a practitioner of the spoils system—to hand out jobs, as was the practice at that time, to his friends and political supporters. But instead, upon the passage of the Pendleton Act—the bill that initiated the modern civil service system—Arthur not only signed it but also fully enforced it. He further angered his old friends and supporters by vetoing the River and Harbors Act, a $19-million piece of pork-barrel legislation.

In 1882 Arthur created a tariff commission, which recommended that duties be cut sharply; however, lobbyists succeeded in diluting the resulting legislation to the extent that the new tariffs were only reduced by a small percentage.

Also in 1882, Arthur vetoed legislation that called for an outright ban on Chinese immigration for twenty years; he later signed a law that shortened the term of suspension to ten years.

His courageous political acts—especially in the enforcement of civil-service reform and the vetoing of pork-barrel legislation—cost him his anticipated renomination in 1884. The Republican party turned its back on the sitting president.

Arthur returned to private law practice but, having long suffered from Bright's disease (a kidney ailment), he saw his health rapidly deteriorate. He died within two years of retirement from the presidency, on November 18, 1886, at his home in New York City.

☆ ☆ ☆

I may be President of the United States, but my private life is nobody's damned business.

The Office of Vice-President is a greater honor than I ever dreamed of attaining.

All personal considerations and political views must be merged in the national sorrow. I am an American among millions grieving for their wounded chief.
(on the assassination of President James Garfield)

Men may die, but the fabrics of our free institutions remain unshaken.

No higher or more assuring proof could exist of the strength and permanence of popular government than the fact that though the chosen of the people be struck down his constitutional successor is peacefully installed without shock or strain except the sorrow which mourns the bereavement.
(on the assassination of President James Garfield)

If it were not for the reporters, I would tell you the truth.

Well, there doesn't seem to be anything else for an ex-president to do but go into the country and raise big pumpkins.

☆ GROVER CLEVELAND ☆

22nd and 24th President

Birth: March 18, 1837   Death: June 24, 1908
Terms: March 4, 1885–March 3, 1889
March 4, 1893–March 3, 1897

THE CLEVELAND PRESIDENCIES

- *Chicago World's Fair opens (1893)*
- *Panic of 1893*
- *Pullman strike (1894)*
- *Utah admitted as forty-fifth state (1896)*

When in 1893 a cancerous growth was discovered on the roof of President Grover Cleveland's mouth, a secret—because Cleveland feared that worries over his health would worsen an already gloomy economic situation—hour-long operation was performed by Dr. Joseph Bryant on a yacht cruising in the East River off Manhattan. Bryant successfully removed the president's left upper jaw and part of his palate and fitted Cleveland with an artificial jaw of vulcanized rubber (all surgery was done from within the mouth to avoid an external scar). The facts of the case did not come out until well after Cleveland's death, when, in 1917, Dr. W. W. Keen, one of the physicians present at the secretive surgery, told the world of the clandestine boat ride.

When Cleveland, the son of a Presbyterian minister, was four, his family moved from Caldwell, New Jersey (his birthplace), to Fayetteville, New York. A decade later, they moved again, to Clinton, New York. A hardworking student, he hoped to go to college, but his father's death when Cleveland was sixteen made his wish a financial impossibility. After several odd jobs, he headed for Cleveland, Ohio, because he liked the name of the city. On the way he stopped to visit an uncle in Buffalo, and there he stayed, working in an attorney's office while studying law. In 1859, he was admitted to the New York bar.

In 1861, upon the outbreak of the Civil War, Cleveland was drafted. He chose to purchase a substitute, a legal option at that time, paying $150 to a thirty-two-year-old Polish immigrant to serve in his place.

Cleveland served as sheriff of Erie County, mayor of Buffalo, and governor of New York. Nominated by the Democrats for president in 1884, he brought to the race a strong and well-earned reputation for honesty, eliminating government corruption, and cutting taxes. His campaign also brought another issue center stage: the charge that Cleveland had fathered an illegitimate son, born in 1874 to Maria Halpin, a Buffalo department store clerk. Asked by his political handlers how to respond to the charges, he boldly instructed them to tell the truth—that he had fathered the child. His candid admission caught the fancy of the public and did much to defuse what could have been a far more damaging issue. Cleveland won a very close election—a switch of just 528 votes in New York would have caused him to lose.

In 1886 when he (age forty-nine) married Frances Folsom (twenty-one), he became the first president to be married in the White House. His wife—the youngest First Lady ever—was of great interest to the press and its readers. The couple silently suffered from baseless gossip that she was physically abused by Cleveland. After his defeat in the election of 1888, the First Lady warned the White House staff that she would return in four years. She was proved right.

The election of 1888 was another close one. Although Cleveland won the popular vote, Benjamin Harrison won the electoral college. Had Cleveland only carried his home state of New York, he would have won the election.

Four years later, in 1892, when Cleveland again ran against Harrison, the campaign was dominated by the tariff issue. Harrison defended the protectionist McKinley Tariff whereas Cleveland, while assuring voters that he opposed absolute free trade, continued his efforts for a reduction in the tariff.

The campaign abruptly turned somber upon the sudden death of First Lady Caroline Harrison. Both candidates ceased to campaign in October. This time, Cleveland won.

Cleveland's presidencies were dominated by economic issues—from the Panic of 1893, which kicked off a four-year depression, to the Pullman Strike of 1894 in which the president used federal militia to break the railroad strike.

Cleveland was one of the country's hardest-working presidents; he stayed in his office night after night until 2 or 3 A.M., reading through hundreds of documents and thousands of pages of legislation. While he signed 1,543 bills, he vetoed hundreds.

Upon his retirement in 1897, Cleveland became an active trustee of Princeton University, where his opinions on school policy often clashed with those of its president, Woodrow Wilson. He wrote articles for the *Saturday Evening Post* and served as a consultant to the insurance industry.

In 1908, after months of failing health, Cleveland died of heart failure. His last words were: "I have tried so hard to do right."

☆　☆　☆

I am honest and sincere in my desire to do well, but the question is whether I know enough to accomplish what I desire.

The farmer's son, not satisfied with his father's simple and laborious life, joins the eager chase for easily acquired wealth.

The truly American sentiment recognizes the dignity of labor and the fact that honor lies in natural toil.

This dreadful, damnable office-seeking hangs over me and surrounds me—and makes me feel like resigning.

This office seeking is a disease. It is even catching.

Must we always look for the political opinions of our business men precisely where they suppose their immediate pecuniary advantage is found?

A man is known by the company he keeps, and also by the company from which he is kept out.

Sensible and responsible women do not want to vote.

I feel like a locomotive hitched to a boy's express wagon.
(on how it felt to be without the burden of the presidency)

He who takes the oath today to preserve, protect, and defend the Constitution of the United States only assumes the solemn obligation which every patriotic citizen . . . should share with him. . . . Your every voter, as surely as your Chief Magistrate, under the same high sanction, though in a different sphere, exercises a public trust.

The lessons of paternalism ought to be unlearned and the better lesson taught that while the people should patriotically and cheerfully support their Government its functions do not include the support of the people.

The admitted right of a government to prevent the influx of elements hostile to its internal peace and security may not be questioned, even where there is not treaty stipulation on the subject. *(on immigration)*

Party honesty is party expediency.

Ours is not a government which operates well by its own momentum. It is so constructed that it will only yield its best results when it feels the constant pressure of the hands of the people.

He mocks the people who proposes that the government shall protect the rich and that they in turn will care for the laboring poor.

Every citizen owes to the country a vigilant watch and close scrutiny of its public servants and affairs and a reasonable estimate of their fidelity and usefulness.

What is the use of being elected or reelected, unless you stand for something?

☆ BENJAMIN HARRISON ☆

23rd President

Birth: August 20, 1833   Death: March 13, 1901
Term: March 4, 1889–March 3, 1893

THE HARRISON (BENJAMIN) PRESIDENCY

- *Sherman Anti-Trust Act enacted (1890)*
- *Montana (1889), Washington (1889), South Dakota (1889), North Dakota (1889), Wyoming (1890), and Idaho (1890) admitted as states*
- *First president to sign papers by electric light (1891)*
- *Last president with a beard*

In 1891, when the Edison company installed electricity in the White House for the first time, the Harrisons were so fearful of the new device that they refused to touch switches; they would sleep through the night with all the lights burning, waiting until the White House engineer came back on duty in the morning.

Benjamin Harrison was born in North Bend, Ohio, into politics: his father—the only man to be both the son of one president and the father of another—was a congressman from Ohio; his grandfather was William Henry Harrison, the ninth president; and his great-grandfather signed the Declaration of Independence.

An excellent student, Harrison's lifelong flair for public speaking—his idol was Patrick Henry—first surfaced while a student at Miami (Ohio) University where he was elected president of the Union Literary Society, joined the Phi Delta Theta fraternity, and delivered one of the commencement addresses at his

116

graduation. He studied law in Cincinnati and was admitted to the bar in 1854. In the same year, he moved to Indianapolis where he formed a law partnership.

In 1853, at age twenty and after a courtship of six years, he married Caroline Lavinia Scott, age twenty-one. When the Harrisons reached Washington, the First Lady secured $35,000 from Congress to renovate the White House, including the extermination of its heavy rodent and insect populations. Sadly, during her husband's campaign for reelection, the First Lady developed tuberculosis and died just two weeks prior to the election, leaving her husband, a son, and a daughter.

Four years later, at the age of sixty-two, Harrison married Mary Scott Lord Dimmick, a thirty-seven-year-old widow. They had one daughter.

Although modest about his Civil War service—"I am not a Julius Caesar, nor a Napoleon, but a plain Hoosier colonel, with no more relish for a fight than for a good breakfast and hardly so much"— he rose from second lieutenant to brigadier general. Harrison, among the first Union soldiers to march into Atlanta when it finally fell, was cited for his foresight, discipline, and fighting spirit.

He served as a U.S. senator from Indiana prior to his election to the presidency. The tariff issue dominated his first presidential campaign, with Harrison promising a strong, protective tariff to safeguard domestic industry and his opponent, Grover Cleveland, proposing a tariff reduction.

A longtime champion of his fellow veterans, in 1890 Harrison enthusiastically signed the Dependent and Disability Pensions Act which extended compensation to veterans disabled from nonmilitary causes and to their dependents. In the same year, he also approved the Sherman Anti-Trust Act, which was the first of many antitrust laws to attempt to curb the abuses of monopolies.

In 1890, Harrison signed the McKinley Tariff Act, a severely protective measure that set the average tariff rate at 48 percent, the highest ever in peacetime, up to that point in the Union's history. The tariff was not universally popular as it caused drastic increases in the cost of many imported agricultural products like sugar and most items that were not manufactured domestically. It was this high tariff that ultimately led to Harrison's defeat in the Harrison-Cleveland rematch election of 1892.

In retirement, the twenty-third president practiced law, wrote, served as a diplomat, and actively supported various political candidates and causes. He died of pneumonia on March 13, 1901.

☆ ☆ ☆

When I came into power, I found that the party managers had taken it all to themselves. I could not name my own Cabinet. They sold out every place to pay the election expenses.

The manner by which women are treated is a good criterion to judge the true state of society. If we know but this one feature in a character of a nation, we may easily judge the rest, for as society advances, the true character of women is discovered.

Have you not learned that not stocks or bonds or stately homes or products of mill or field are our country? It is the splendid thought that is in our minds.

The Yankee intermingles with the Illinoisian, the Hoosier with the Sucker, and the people of the South with them all and it is this commingling which gives that unity which marks the American nation.

The applicants for office are generally respectable and worthy men . . . but at the end of one hundred days of this work the President should not be judged too harshly if he shows a little wear, a little loss of effusiveness, and even a hunted expression in his eyes.

And we must not forget that it is often easier to assemble armies than it is to assemble army revenues.

If we bar out the irresponsible crank, so far as I can see the President is in no peril, except that he may be killed by the superabundant kindness of the people.

I said to one of the first delegations that visited me that this was a contest of great principles; that it would be fought out upon the high plains of truth, and not in the swamps of slander and defamation. Those who will encamp their army in the swamp will abandon the victory to the army that is on the heights.

What questions are we to grapple with? What unfinished work remains to be done? It seems to me that the work that is unfinished is to make that constitutional grant of citizenship, the franchise to the colored men of the South, a practical and living reality.

I believe also in the American opportunity which puts the starry sky above every boy's head, and sets his foot upon a ladder which he may climb until his strength gives out.

Some of us fancied that the Southern people were given to vaporizing—that each one of them was equal to five Northern soldiers. But the South learned that Paul Revere still rode the highways of Massachusetts, and that the man of Concord still plowed the fields. And we, on our part, learned that the spirit of the cavalier which was found in the Southern army was combined with the reserve and steadfastness of Cromwell's Ironsides.

Unlike many other people less happy, we give our devotion to a Government, to its Constitution, to its flag, and not to men.

Lincoln had faith in time, and time has justified his faith.

Mobs do not discriminate, and the punishments inflicted by them have no repressive or salutary influence.

We Americans have no commission from God to police the world.

As to the baby, I told his mother to say to him that if he would be patient until the snow is gone, we would all move out on the roof and give him the house.
(about his first grandchild)

We cannot afford in America to have any discontented classes, and if fair wages are paid for fair work we will have none.

☆ WILLIAM MCKINLEY ☆

25th President

Birth: January 29, 1843   Death: September 14, 1901
Term: March 4, 1897–September 4, 1901

THE MCKINLEY PRESIDENCY

- *United States declares war on Spain (1898)*

- *Treaty of Paris ends Spanish-American War (1898)*

- *Hawaii, Guam, Puerto Rico, the Philippines, and American Samoa acquired (1899)*

Many of his contemporaries remarked on William McKinley's deep devotion to his wife. She had become totally dependent upon him when she developed epilepsy following a nervous breakdown caused by the deaths of their only two children in infancy. Whenever she had a seizure in public (she had one at McKinley's inaugural ball), McKinley would gently place a handkerchief over her face to conceal her contorted features. Once the seizure passed, he would remove the handkerchief and continue with the occasion at hand, as if nothing had happened. Mark Hanna, McKinley's campaign manager, noted, "President McKinley had made it pretty bad for the rest of us husbands in Washington."

The twenty-fifth president was born in Niles, Ohio, a town of about three hundred people. When he was nine, the family moved to Poland, Ohio, which wasn't much bigger. A good student and a naturally gifted orator, he helped organize and direct his school's literary and debating societies. He studied for a year at Allegheny

College in Meadville, Pennsylvania, but was forced to drop out for health reasons (physical exhaustion from excessive studying).

McKinley then served (1861–65) in the Civil War with the Twenty-third Ohio Volunteer Infantry, rising from private to major. After the war he studied law, was admitted to the Ohio bar in 1867, and began the process of realizing his life's dream—the presidency:

I have never been in doubt since I was old enough to think intelligently that I would someday be made President.

McKinley served several terms as a U.S. representative and as governor of Ohio prior to his run for the presidency in 1896. The Republicans nominated him on the first ballot. Like Benjamin Harrison, McKinley ran a "front porch" campaign: he refused to leave his wife's side to travel around the country, so his supporters—including some of the nation's wealthiest citizens—were brought to McKinley's home where the front porch served as the setting for their discussions. The 1896 race pitted McKinley, generously supported by wealthy industrialists, against William Jennings Bryan, an energetic populist; it was the first election to cast the country's immigrant masses against the privileged class.

McKinley's presidency was dominated by the Spanish-American War, a conflict that McKinley entered only reluctantly, despite the persistence of the "yellow press," which fed the flames of hatred with anti-Spanish articles, many of which were simply not true. America was "feeling its oats," with many of its citizens eager for conflict. A natural antipathy toward a European power trying to maintain colonies in the Western Hemisphere (specifically, in Cuba) combined with reports of Spanish atrocities against Cubans stirred Americans to battle. When the United States battleship *Maine* exploded and sank in Havana harbor, Spain was blamed although the cause of the explosion was never determined. The war cry "Remember the *Maine*! To Hell with Spain!" energized the prowar forces, and McKinley and Congress eventually acceded. Four months later, the Spanish armies in the Philippines, Cuba, and Puerto Rico were defeated and the Spanish navy was destroyed. The war was over and an expansionist United States now controlled the Philippines, Guam, and Puerto Rico.

That same expansionist spirit spearheaded the annexation of Hawaii and became a contentious issue in the election of 1900 in which McKinley pursued reelection, once again opposed by William Jennings Bryan. Bryan charged that McKinley's United States was becoming an imperial power, bent on acquiring far-flung colonies. The president countered, claiming that as an emerging world power, the United States had a responsibility to bring civilization and the American way to backward peoples. He won, with a larger margin of victory over Bryan than four years earlier.

On September 6, 1901, as McKinley greeted people at the Pan-American Exposition in Buffalo, a young, self-avowed anarchist by the name of Leon Czolgosz approached the president and shot him twice. As he fell to the ground, his thoughts immediately turned to his wife: "My wife," he whispered to a nearby friend, "be careful, how you tell her—oh, be careful."

McKinley died eight days later.

☆ ☆ ☆

I am a tariff man, standing on a tariff platform.

That's all a man can hope for during his lifetime—to set an example—and when he is dead, to be an inspiration to history.

We need Hawaii just as much and a good deal more than we did California. It is Manifest Destiny.

If old Dewey had just sailed away when he smashed the Spanish fleet, what a lot of trouble he would have saved us.
(*on taking possession of the Philippines*)

We want no war of conquest . . . War should never be entered upon until every agency of peace has failed.

I have already transmitted to Congress the report of the naval court of inquiry on the destruction of the battleship *Maine* in the harbor of Havana during the night of the fifteenth of February. The destruction of that noble vessel has filled the national heart with inexpressible horror. Two hundred and fifty-eight brave sailors and marines and two officers of our Navy, reposing in the fancied security of a friendly harbor, have been hurled to death, grief and want brought to their homes and sorrow to the nation.

I have no enemies. Why should I fear?
(*on assassination*)

Illiteracy must be banished from the land if we shall attain that high destiny as the foremost of the enlightened nations of the world which, under Providence, we ought to achieve.

There was nothing left for us to do but to take them all, and to educate the Filipinos, and uplift and civilize and Christianize them, and by God's grace do the very best we could do for them, as our fellow-men for whom Christ also died.
(*on his decision to take claim of the Philippine Islands*)

Benevolent assimilation.
(*on colonialism*)

Our differences are policies, our agreements principles.

In the time of darkest defeat, victory may be nearest.

The best way for the Government to maintain its credit is to pay as it goes—not by resorting to loans, but by keeping out of debt —through an adequate income secured by a system of taxation, external or internal, or both.

Good-bye—good-bye, all. It's God's way. His will, not ours, be done. Nearer, my God, to Thee, nearer to Thee.
(his last words)

☆ THEODORE ROOSEVELT ☆

26th President

Birth: October 27, 1858   Death: January 6, 1919
Term: September 14, 1901–March 3, 1909

THE ROOSEVELT (THEODORE) PRESIDENCY

- *First wireless signal received from Europe (1901)*
- *Panama Canal Zone acquired (1904)*
- *The great San Francisco earthquake and fire (1906)*
- *Oklahoma admitted as forty-sixth state (1907)*

Active, energized, and the youngest president yet at age forty-two, Roosevelt was a great proponent of the outdoor, recreational, and sporting lives. He even boxed in the White House gym, once going a few rounds with heavyweight champion John L. Sullivan, who scored a hard blow to the president's face. The punch permanently blinded Roosevelt's left eye, which remained a well-kept secret for years, because Roosevelt feared the humiliation that might result from the news that the president had been so seriously injured during a simple sparring session in the White House basement.

The only president born in New York City, Roosevelt was a sickly child, suffering severely from asthma, safely sleeping only when propped up in bed. He fought back, though, exercising endlessly, swimming and lifting weights, developing a deep chest, powerful arms and shoulders, and great endurance which lasted a lifetime (after a busy day, he used to get up from his White House desk and run several laps around the Washington Monument to work off excess energy). Too sick to attend school, Roosevelt was tutored until admitted to Harvard. There he excelled in extracurricular activities, sports, and studies. He then entered Columbia Law School but dropped out to run for the state assembly. He never sought admission to the bar.

Roosevelt, twenty-two, married Alice Hathaway Lee, nineteen, in 1880. On their fourth anniversary, she died from complications of childbirth. On the same day, in the same house, Roosevelt's mother also died. Roosevelt was crushed. He left his infant daughter with an aunt and moved to the Dakota Territory where he bought a ranch and for two years worked as a cowboy. "There were all kinds of things," he said, "of which I was afraid at first . . . from grizzly bears to 'mean' horses and gunfighters; but by acting as if I were not afraid, I gradually ceased to be afraid."

At age twenty-eight he returned to New York City and married Edith Kermit Carow, twenty-five. Their relationship proved to be more a jovial friendship than a passionate romance, although it produced another five children. Roosevelt's six children brought new life to the White House, where the kids walked on stilts, slid down banisters, and even took their pony upstairs in the elevator.

In 1886, Roosevelt's political career began in defeat with a failed campaign for mayor of New York City. He then served on the U.S. Civil Service Commission, as president of the New York City Police Board (where his growing public persona benefited from his effective campaign to root out police corruption), as assistant secretary of the navy, and as governor of New York.

He was chosen by professional political hacks to fill the vice presidential slot on a ticket with President McKinley principally to get his honesty and reformist influence out of New York. As vice president, it was assumed, he would be out of the way with little to do. But upon McKinley's assassination, "that damned cowboy," as one of his political enemies complained, "is now President of the United States."

Roosevelt had secured the status of popular hero during the

Spanish-American War when he served as commander of the First
U.S. Volunteer Cavalry Regiment—popularly known as the Rough
Riders. At San Juan, Roosevelt and his Rough Riders distinguished
themselves, electrifying the nation in a reportedly valiant charge:
"I would rather have led that charge and earned my colonelcy than
served three times in the United States Senate."

In his first message to Congress in 1901, Roosevelt set forth his
antitrust policy. He believed that many of America's great businesses, by joining together in "trusts," were eliminating competition so that people would be forced to work at low wages or not
at all. Roosevelt feared that this widening gap between the wealthy
few and the numerous poor was as dangerous to the endurance of
the nation as was the South/North split of forty years earlier. The
Roosevelt administration brought suit under the antitrust laws
against the railroad, beef, oil, tobacco, and other industries. His
antitrust policies, his advocacy of labor interests, and his support
for consumer rights became known as the "Square Deal."

Roosevelt was the first president to value the country's natural
resources *and* do something about it—his administration established more than 125 million acres of national forests.

He was determined to see a canal built across Central America
to facilitate shipping from coast to coast. When he found it impossible to purchase the necessary land and rights, the Roosevelt
administration, in concert with certain business interests, provoked
a revolution in Panama—then controlled by Colombia—to create
a government that would grant the president his wish.

Roosevelt declined to seek reelection in 1908, as he had promised he would during the election of 1904. In retirement he remained, to no one's surprise, active. He traveled around the world
and wrote many articles and books. Breaking his promise in 1912,
he mounted a failed third-party presidential campaign as the nominee of the Progressive Republicans, the "Bull Moose" party (its
platform was less conservative than that of the Taft-led Republican
party).

Ten years after leaving the White House, Roosevelt died uncharacteristically quietly in his sleep. His last words were: "Please put out the light."

☆ ☆ ☆

He is a cold-blooded, narrow-minded, prejudiced, obstinate, timid old psalm-singing Indianapolis politician.
(on Benjamin Harrison)

The most successful politician is he who says what everybody is thinking and in the loudest voice.

No President has ever enjoyed himself as much as I.

He is an utterly selfish and cold-blooded politician always.
(on Woodrow Wilson)

Stand the gaff, play fair; be a good man to camp out with.

Far better it is to dare mighty things, to win glorious triumphs, even though checkered by failure, than to take rank with those poor spirits who neither enjoy much nor suffer much, because they live in the gray twilight that knows not victory nor defeat.

Get action, do things; be sane, don't fritter away your time; create, act, take place wherever you are and be somebody; get action.

The American people are slow to wrath, but when their wrath is once kindled it burns like a consuming flame.

From the beginning our people have markedly combined practical capacity for affairs with power of devotion to an ideal. The lack of either quality would have rendered the possession of the other of small value.

Americanism is a question of principle, of purpose, of Idealism, or Character; it is not a matter of birthplace or creed or line of descent.

The things that will destroy America are prosperity-at-any-price, peace at-any-price, safety-first instead of duty-first, the love of soft living and the get-rich-quick theory of life.

I do not believe there is any danger of any assault upon my life . . . and if there were it would be simple nonsense to try to prevent it, for as Lincoln said, though it would be safer for a President to live in a cage, it would interfere with his business.

Friends, I shall ask you to be as quiet as possible. I don't know whether you fully understand that I have been shot; but it takes more than that to kill a Bull Moose.
(*five minutes after being shot in Milwaukee, Wisconsin, October 14, 1912*)

Actions speak louder than words.

There can be no effective control of corporations while their political activity remains.

We demand that big business give people a square deal; in return we must insist that when anyone engaged in big business honestly endeavors to do right, he himself shall be given a square deal.

If elected, I shall see to it that every man has a square deal, no less and no more.

The New Nationalism puts the national needs before sectional or personal advantage. . . . The man who wrongly holds that every human right is secondary to his profit must now give way to the advocate of human welfare who rightly maintains that every man holds his property subject to the general right of the community to regulate its use to whatever degree the public welfare may require.

My hat's in the ring. The fight is on and I'm stripped to the buff.

I am as strong as a bull moose and you can use me up to the limit.
(at the opening of the campaign of 1912)

No people is wholly civilized where the distinction is drawn between stealing an office and stealing a purse.

The leader works in the open and the boss in covert. The leader leads, and the boss drives.

It was my good fortune at Santiago to serve beside colored troops. A man who is good enough to shed his blood for the country is good enough to be given a square deal afterward. More than that no man is entitled to and less than that no man shall have.

We stand supreme in a Continent, in a hemisphere. East and West we look across two great oceans toward the larger world life in which, whether we will or not, we must take an ever-increasing share.

Our place must be great among the nations. We may either fail greatly or succeed greatly; but we cannot avoid the endeavor from which either great failure or great success must come. Even if we would, we cannot play a small part. If we should try, all that would follow would be that we should play a large part ignobly or shamefully.

I wish that all Americans would realize that American politics is world politics.

Congress does from a third to a half of what I think is the minimum that it ought to do, and I am profoundly grateful that I get as much.

I have a very strong feeling that it is a President's duty to get on with Congress if he possibly can, and that it is a reflection upon him if he and Congress come to a complete break.

The Constitution was made for the people and not the people for the Constitution.

Under government ownership corruption can flourish just as rankly as under private ownership.

It behooves every man to remember that the work of the critic . . . is of altogether secondary importance, and that, in the end, progress is accomplished by the man who does . . . things.

There is no room in this country for hyphenated Americans. . . . The one absolutely certain way of bringing this nation to ruin, of preventing all possibility of it continuing to be a nation at all, would be to permit it to become a tangle of squabbling nationalities.

Probably the greatest harm done by vast wealth is the harm that we of moderate means do ourselves when we let the vices of envy and hatred enter deep into our own nature.

Order without liberty and liberty without order are equally destructive.

The first requisite of a good citizen in this Republic of ours is that he shall be able and willing to pull his weight.

There is a homely adage which runs: "Speak softly and carry a big stick; you will go far." If the American nation will speak softly and yet build and keep at a pitch of the highest training a thoroughly efficient navy, the Monroe Doctrine will go far.

No man is above the law and no man is below it; nor do we ask any man's permission when we require him to obey it. Obedience to the law is demanded as a right; not asked as a favor.

To waste, to destroy our natural resources, to skin and exhaust the land instead of using it so as to increase its usefulness, will result in undermining in the days of our children the very prosperity which we ought by right to hand down to them amplified and developed.

One of our defects as a nation is a tendency to use what have been called "weasel words." When a weasel sucks eggs the meat is sucked out of the egg. If you use a "weasel word" after another there is nothing left of the other.

Every immigrant who comes here should be required within five years to learn English or leave the country.

The man who loves other countries as much as his own stands on a level with the man who loves other women as much as he loves his own wife.

Peace is normally a great good, and normally it coincides with righteousness, but it is righteousness and not peace which should bind the conscience of a nation as it should bind the conscience of an individual; and neither a nation nor an individual can surrender conscience to another's keeping.

A muttonhead, after an education at West Point—or Harvard—is a muttonhead still.

A man who has never gone to school may steal from a freight car; but if he has a university education, he may steal the whole railroad.

No man is justified in doing evil on the ground of expedience.

I never take a step in foreign policy unless I am assured that I shall be able eventually to carry out my will by force.

No man should receive a dollar unless that dollar has been fairly earned. Every dollar received should represent a dollar's worth of service rendered—not gambling in stocks, but services rendered.

Every reform movement has a lunatic fringe.

Please put out the light.
(his last words)

☆ WILLIAM HOWARD TAFT ☆

27th President

Birth: September 15, 1857   Death: March 8, 1930
Term: March 4, 1909–March 3, 1913

THE TAFT PRESIDENCY

• *Peary discovers North Pole (1909)*

• *Cows kept on White House lawn*

• *First President to toss out the first ball on opening day of the baseball season*

• *New Mexico and Arizona admitted as forty-seventh and forty-eighth states (1912)*

• *First president to play golf*

• *Sixteenth Amendment to the Constitution establishes federal income tax (1913)*

• *President gets stuck in White House bathtub and new one— large enough to hold four ordinary men—is installed*

Some president has to be the largest. At six feet, two inches, and as much as 326 pounds, William Howard Taft was that president.

Born in Cincinnati, Taft was a fun-loving and active boy who especially enjoyed baseball—although because of his size, he was an awful base runner. Taft was a good student, always placing at or near the top of his class, from his public-school education in Cincinnati to Yale University and the University of Cincinnati law school. He was admitted to the Ohio bar in 1880.

In 1886, Taft, then twenty-eight, married Helen "Nellie" Herron, twenty-five. Mrs. Taft encouraged her husband's political career, urging him to accept the presidential nomination in 1908 despite his preference for the judiciary (Taft's lifelong ambition was to serve on the Supreme Court).

Nellie was the first wife of a president to ride alongside her husband down Pennsylvania Avenue on Inauguration Day (previously, the new president had always ridden next to the outgoing chief executive). Ironically, Nellie was unable to enjoy the years in the White House, as she suffered a severe stroke in 1909 (during her slow recovery, the president lovingly taught her to speak again). In her most lasting contribution as First Lady, Mrs. Taft arranged for the planting of the three thousand Japanese cherry trees that today grace the Washington Tidal Basin.

Taft's political career was remarkably diverse: he served as assistant prosecutor of Hamilton County (Ohio), collector of internal revenue for Ohio's First District, assistant solicitor of Hamilton County, judge of the Cincinnati Superior Court, U.S. solicitor general, judge of the Sixth U.S. Circuit Court, governor-general of the Philippines, secretary of war, acting secretary of state, and provisional governor of Cuba.

Taft was handpicked by President Theodore Roosevelt—who had pledged not to run again—to succeed him. With a campaign built around extending the popular Roosevelt presidency, Taft easily defeated his Democratic opponent, William Jennings Bryan.

For the most part, Taft succeeded with his intention to carry on Roosevelt's progressive policies. He improved the civil service, and he set aside government-owned lands where oil and coal were found, claiming that the profit from these belonged to the people, not private business. But Taft lacked Roosevelt's flair, and eventually his popularity eroded simply because he wasn't *like* Teddy. Even Teddy turned on Taft. In 1912, Roosevelt formed the Bull Moose party and opposed Taft for reelection along with the Democratic nominee, Woodrow Wilson.

Wilson won the three-way contest, and Taft joyfully returned to his law practice and his teaching: "I am glad to be going. This is the lonesomest place in the world."

In 1921, his lifelong dream was fulfilled—he was happily appointed chief justice of the United States: "I don't even remember that I ever was President."

During his nine years on the bench, he wrote 253 opinions, about one-sixth of all the decisions handed down during his term.

Justice Louis Brandeis said of Taft, "It's very difficult for me to understand how a man who is so good as Chief Justice could have been so bad as President." Taft served as Chief Justice until failing health forced his retirement in 1930.

He died on March 8, 1930. His was the first presidential funeral broadcast on radio.

Politics when I am in it, makes me sick.

I hate to use the patronage as a club unless I have to.

In the days before the present civil service law, a sense of obligation to the President for the places held made practically all the civil employees his political henchmen. In those halcyon times, even the humblest charwoman or the most poorly paid janitor felt a throb of deep personal interest in the political health of the president.

Machine politics and the spoils system are as much an enemy of a proper and efficient government system of civil service as the boll weevil is of the cotton crop.

I am delighted to learn that the dastardly attack was unsuccessful. The resort to violence is out of place in our twentieth-century civilization.
(*on the attempted assassination of Theodore Roosevelt*)

Presidents may go to the seashore or to the mountains, Cabinet Officers may go about the country explaining how fortunate the country is in having such an administration, but the machinery at Washington continues to operate under the army of faithful non-commissioned officers, and the great mass of governmental business is uninterrupted.

Nobody ever drops in for the evening.
(*on life at the White House*)

There is a well-known aphorism that men are different, but all husbands are alike. The same idea may be paraphrased with respect to Congressmen. Congressmen are different, but when in opposition to an administration they are very much alike in their attitude and in their speeches.

I have come to the conclusion that the major part of the work of a President is to increase the gate receipts of expositions and fairs and bring tourists into town.

We live in a stage of politics, where legislators seem to regard the passage of laws as much more important than the results of their enforcement.

A system in which we may have an enforced rest from legislation for two years is not bad.

I am afraid I am a constant disappointment to my party. The fact of the matter is, the longer I am President the less of a party man I seem to become.

Anti-semitism is a noxious weed that should be cut out. It has no place in America.

I am President now, and tired of being kicked around.

I'll be damned if I am not getting tired of this. It seems to be the profession of a President simply to hear other people talk.

Substantial progress toward better things can rarely be taken without developing new evils requiring new remedies.

Next to the right of liberty, the right of property is the most important individual right guaranteed by the Constitution and the one which, united with that of personal liberty, has contributed more to the growth of civilization than any other institution established by the human race.

☆ WOODROW WILSON ☆

28th President

Birth: December 28, 1856   Death: February 3, 1924
Term: March 4, 1913–March 3, 1921

THE WILSON PRESIDENCY

• *German submarine sinks* Lusitania *(1915)*

• *United States purchases Virgin Islands (1917)*

• *United States declares war on Germany (1917)*

• *World War I ends (1918)*

• *Women given right to vote (Nineteenth Amendment, 1920)*

A year after his first wife, Ellen Louise Axson, died in the White House, Woodrow Wilson escorted Edith Galt, a widow, to the theater. *The Washington Post* reported that instead of watching the performance, "the President spent most of his time entering Mrs. Galt."

It was an embarrassing typographical error. The sentence was intended to read "entertaining" Mrs. Galt.

Wilson was born on December 28, 1856, in Staunton, Virginia. Both his father and grandfather were Presbyterian ministers, and many said that Woodrow "looked like a preacher" with his high forehead, thin nose, and firm mouth. Within a year of his birth, the family moved to Augusta, Georgia. Wilson's childhood, then, included a keen awareness of the humiliation and devastation of the post–Civil War South. From these roots grew his lifelong belief that the South was totally justified in seceding from the Union. He also believed in white supremacy.

Wilson eventually studied law, although he never enjoyed its practice as much as he did its appropriateness for launching a political career.

In 1885, Wilson, age twenty-eight, married Ellen Louise Axson, twenty-five, the daughter of a Presbyterian minister. She gave birth to three children. Wilson's devotion to Ellen was passionate and obsessive and when she died of Bright's disease at the White House in August of 1914, he sat beside her body for two full days, coming close to a serious breakdown and even confiding to an aide that he hoped to be assassinated.

Wilson's career, unlike most of his presidential predecessors, was rooted in academia. He taught at Bryn Mawr College and Wesleyan University, lectured at Johns Hopkins University, and settled into a professorship at Princeton. His political and historical works earned him a national reputation for insightful scholarship. He became Princeton's president in 1902 and served in that capacity until elected governor of New Jersey in 1910. Two years later the Democrats nominated him for the presidency. Wilson won the election when the opposing Republican vote was split between the incumbent, Taft, and former president Theodore Roosevelt, who ran as a third-party candidate.

Wilson believed that the job of the president was to represent everybody (unlike members of Congress, who represented special areas and interests). Wilson's progressive, pro-labor presidency included acts to lower tariffs, revise the national banking system, shorten the working day to eight hours, allow smaller businesses to compete more fairly with larger ones, and minimize the likelihood of monopolies.

A year and a half after his first wife's death, Wilson, then fifty-eight, married the widowed Mrs. Edith Bolling Galt, forty-three. In the same year he ran for reelection with the campaign slogan

"He kept us out of war." But soon after his successful reelection, German submarines began to sink American ships in the Atlantic Ocean. Wilson finally asked Congress to declare war against Germany.

Wilson hoped that World War I would be the "war to end all wars." Even while the fighting raged, he worked on long-range peace plans, which he set forth to Congress as "Fourteen Points." The Fourteenth Point called for a League of Nations—an impartial organization of all nations which would peacefully settle future arguments among countries.

Wilson committed himself to promoting U.S. participation in the League. He embarked on an exhausting national tour, speaking in twenty-nine cities in three weeks. It proved to be too much. He suffered a physical breakdown and, days later, a stroke from which he never fully recovered. Worse yet for Wilson, in the end, the U.S. Senate failed to approve joining the proposed League of Nations and the great concept failed, only to be resurrected in spirit after World War II as the United Nations.

Upon his stroke, Wilson's wife effectively took over the presidency for the next seventeen months, until the end of his second term. Some members of Congress were not so pleased by the arrangement, claiming "We have a petticoat government! Mrs. Wilson is President!"

Wilson and his wife retired to a newly purchased home in Washington, D.C., where he attempted to practice law although his failing health greatly limited his activities. He died on February 3, 1924. He spoke his last public words in November 1923:

I am not one of those that have the least anxiety about the triumph of the principles I have stood for: I have seen fools resist Providence before, and I have seen their destruction, as will come upon these again, utter destruction and contempt. That we shall prevail is as sure as that God reigns.

☆ ☆ ☆

He combined great gifts with great mediocrity.
(on Ulysses S. Grant)

It is only working with an energy which is almost superhuman and looks to uninterested spectators like insanity that we can accomplish anything worth the achievement.

Life does not consist in thinking, it consists in acting.

Every man who takes office in Washington either grows or swells, and when I give a man an office, I watch him carefully to see whether he is swelling or growing.

America is not a mere body of traders; it is a body of free men. Our greatness is built upon our freedom—is mortal, not material. We have a great ardor for gain; but we have a deep passion for the rights of man.

I am not one of those who believe that a great standing army is the means of maintaining peace, because if you build up a great profession those who form parts of it want to exercise their profession.

I have sometimes heard men say politics must have nothing to do with business, and I have often wished that business had nothing to do with politics.

The truth is, we are all caught in a great economic system which is heartless.

A general association of nations must be formed under specific covenants for the purpose of affording mutual guarantees of political independence and territorial integrity to great and small states alike.
(the last of the Fourteen Points)

Business underlies everything in our national life, including our spiritual life. Witness the fact that in the Lord's Prayer, the first petition is for daily bread. No one can worship God or love his neighbor on an empty stomach.

There was a time when corporations played a minor part in our business affairs, but now they play the chief part, and most men are the servants of corporations.

If you want to make enemies, try to change something.

There is here a great melting pot in which we must compound a precious metal. That metal is the metal of nationality.

Conservatism is the policy of "make no change and consult your grandmother when in doubt."

The Constitution was not made to fit us like a straitjacket. In its elasticity lies its chief greatness.

The Constitution of the United States is not a mere lawyers' document; it is a vehicle of life, and its spirit is always the spirit of the age.

There is something better, if possible, that a man can give than his life. That is his living spirit to a service that is not easy, to resist counsels that are hard to resist, to stand against purposes that are difficult to stand against.

Caution is the confidential agent of selfishness.

One cool judgement is worth a thousand hasty counsels. The thing to do is to supply light and not heat.

Sometimes people call me an idealist. Well, that is the way I know I am an American . . . America is the only idealist Nation in the world.

Some Americans need hyphens in their names, because only part of them has come over; but when the whole man has come over, heart and thought and all, the hyphen drops of its own weight out of his name.

Gossip: sociologists on a mean and petty scale.

We are constantly thinking of the great war . . . which saved the Union . . . but it was a war that did a great deal more than that. It created in this country what had never existed before—a national consciousness. It was not the salvation of the Union, it was the rebirth of the Union.

I believe in democracy because it releases the energies of every human being.

I am all kinds of a democrat, so far as I can discover—but the root of the whole business is this, that I believe in the patriotism and energy and initiative of the average man.

The beauty of a democracy is that you never can tell when a youngster is born what he is going to do with himself, and that no matter how humbly he is born, no matter where he is born, no matter what circumstances hamper him at the outset, he has got a chance to master the minds and lead the imagination of the whole country.

The use of a university is to make young gentlemen as unlike their fathers as possible.

If I am to speak for ten minutes, I need a week for preparation; if fifteen minutes, three days; if half an hour, two days; if an hour, I am ready now.

Liberty has never come from the government. Liberty has always come from the subjects of it. The history of liberty is a history of resistance. The history of liberty is a history of limitations of governmental power, not the increase of it.

There is a price which it is too great to pay for peace, and that price can be put in one word. One cannot pay the price of self-respect.

Open covenants of peace, openly arrived at.
(*the beginning of his Fourteen Points*)

Things get very lonely in Washington sometimes. The real voice of the great people of America sometimes sounds faint and distant in that strange city. You hear politics until you wish that both parties were smothered in their own gas.

The world must be made safe for democracy. Its peace must be planted upon the tested foundations of political liberty. We have no selfish ends to serve. We desire no conquest, no dominion. We seek no indemnities for ourselves, no material compensation for the sacrifices we shall freely make.
(*address to Congress, 1917, asking for a declaration of war*)

I tell you, fellow citizens, that the war was won by the American spirit. . . . You know what one of our American wits said, that it

took only half as long to train an American army as any other, because we only had to train them to go one way.
(on World War I)

The wisest thing to do with a fool is to encourage him to hire a hall and discourse to his fellow citizens. Nothing chills nonsense like exposure to air.

If you think too much about being reelected, it is very difficult to be worth reelecting.

The great curse of public life is that you are not allowed to say all the things that you think.

The literary gift is a very dangerous gift to possess if you are not telling the truth, and I would a great deal rather, for my part, have a man stumble in his speech than to feel he was so exceedingly smooth that he had better be watched both day and night.

It's harder for a leader to be born in a palace than to be born in a cabin.

The seed of revolution is repression.

WARREN GAMALIEL

☆ HARDING ☆

29th President

Birth: November 2, 1865   Death: August 2, 1923
Term: March 4, 1921–August 2, 1923

THE HARDING PRESIDENCY

- *First female senator, Rebecca L. Felton, appointed (1922)*

- *United States, Japan, Italy, Great Britain, and France sign limitation agreement on naval armaments (1922)*

Despite the generally hostile attitude of liberal historians, it must be conceded that Warren G. Harding actually did more than any other president to preserve the Constitution of the United States. He removed it from the files of the State Department where it had been rotting and had it placed in a protective glass case.

Born in Corsica (later known as Blooming Grove), Ohio, Harding was the son of a poor Ohio farmer and part-time veterinarian who later turned, with no additional training, to the doctoring of people. After graduating from Ohio Central College at age sixteen, Harding worked at odd jobs—teaching school, selling insurance, and organizing the town band—until he and two friends each put up $100 to buy the bankrupt local newspaper, the Marion *Star* (Harding later won controlling interest of the newspaper in a poker game). The newspaper soon prospered with his self-proclaimed editorial policy of "inoffensivism" and his instructions that the name of every man, woman, and child in town should be mentioned in the paper at least once a year.

Elected state senator in 1899, he served as lieutenant governor of Ohio before being elected to the U.S. Senate in 1914.

At the age of twenty-five, Harding married Florence Kling DeWolfe, a homely, domineering, and temperamental divorcée. They never had children. In 1905, while his wife was briefly hospitalized, Harding began a passionate affair with Carrie Philips, the wife of one of his good friends. This romance—which is well documented by over two hundred letters in Harding's handwriting—continued over a period of fifteen years. When that affair ended, he took up with twenty-year-old Nan Britton.

Harding and Miss Britton had a daughter, Elizabeth Ann Christian. Their affair continued throughout Harding's presidency, their favorite hideaway being a small clothes closet adjoining the president's office. (Harding's father once warned him, "If you were a girl, Warren, you'd be in the family way all the time. You can't say no.")

As a senator, Harding's record was undistinguished, but out of a smoke-filled room at the deadlocked Republican convention in 1920, Harding emerged as a compromise candidate. The Republicans employed a simple campaign strategy: keep Harding at home in Marion. As Pennsylvania Senator Boies Penrose noted, "If Warren goes out on tour, somebody's sure to ask him questions, and Warren's just the sort of damned fool that will try to answer them." The campaign resulted in the greatest landslide in the history of American politics up to that time: Harding won 16,153,785 votes to the 9,147,353 garnered by James M. Cox, a Democrat from Ohio. It was the first election in which women voted.

Harding was the first president to ride to his inauguration in an automobile, and his swearing-in was the first described over radio. One astonished British reporter summed up Harding's inaugural address as "the most illiterate statement ever made by the head of a civilized government." Treasury Secretary William G. McAdoo said of Harding, "His speeches left the impression of pompous phrases moving over the landscape in search of an idea. Sometimes these meandering words would actually capture a straggling thought and bear it triumphantly, a prisoner in their midst, until it died of servitude and overwork."

All members of Harding's Cabinet became participants in the president's twice-a-week poker games. Harding would say:

> Forget that I'm President of the United States, I'm Warren Harding, playing poker with friends, and I'm going to beat hell out of them.

Mrs. Harding was generally on hand to mix drinks for the poker players though under the recently passed Prohibition amendment, such refreshments were strictly illegal.

In a 1920 speech, Harding mispronounced the word *normality* and out came *normalcy*. Reporters picked up on *normalcy*, editorial writers commented on it, and the Republicans even came to use the term for political campaigns. "Back to Normalcy" was a call for an idealized nineteenth-century America in which small-town virtues prevailed.

Harding's short presidency was relatively inactive and undistinguished. Content to follow the leadership of Congress on most matters, he vetoed fewer bills than any other president in the twentieth century: six (none was overridden). His secretary of the interior, Albert B. Fall, was convicted of bribery and was the first Cabinet officer in history to go to jail. Harding did persuade the steel industry to reduce the man-killing grind of the twelve-hour day to eight hours, and other industries followed suit. He also advocated civil rights, reduced the national debt, cut taxes significantly, and hastened the release of Eugene V. Debs, a socialist leader imprisoned for antiwar activities.

During Harding's presidency, the Bureau of the Budget was established; the United States, Great Britain, Japan, France, and

Italy agreed to an arms limitation; and the Emergency Tariff Act of 1921 and the Fordney-McCumber Tariff Act of 1922 were passed, raising duties on American industries that had emerged during the war, including the chemical and drug industries.

Alice Roosevelt Longworth—the daughter of President Theodore Roosevelt, wife of Speaker of the House Nicholas Longworth, and, until her death in 1980, a popular society hostess famous for her biting wit and known as "Washington's Other Monument"— said of the Harding presidency: "No rumor could have exceeded the reality in the White House; the study was filled with cronies, the air heavy with tobacco smoke, trays with bottles containing every imaginable brand of whiskey stood about, cards and poker chips ready at hand—a general atmosphere of waist-coat unbuttoned, feet on the desk, and the spittoon alongside."

Harding, the sixth president to die in office, passed away soon after an exhausting cross-country tour when he suffered what was probably a heart attack, incorrectly diagnosed by his personal physician as ptomaine poisoning. The cause of death, however, was never *firmly* established because Mrs. Harding refused to permit an autopsy, fueling speculation that she had poisoned him in revenge for his marital infidelities.

America's present need is not heroics, but healing; not nostrums, but normalcy; not revolution, but restoration; not agitation, but adjustment; not surgery, but serenity; not the dramatic, but the dispassionate; not experiment, but equipoise; not submergence in internationality, but sustainment in triumphant nationality.

I am a man of limited talents from a small town. I don't seem to grasp that I am President.

Government after all is a very simple thing.

I am not fit for this office and never should have been here.
(on the presidency)

I love to meet people. It is the most pleasant thing I do; it is really the only fun I have. It does not tax me, and it seems to be a very great pleasure to them.

American business is not a monster, but an expression of God-given impulse to create, and the savior of our happiness.

Let the black man vote when he is fit to vote, prohibit the white man voting when he is unfit to vote.

It isn't fair. This premature criticism [that he was getting "pouty"] is a serious menace to popular government.

I don't know much about Americanism, but it's a damn good word with which to carry an election.

In the great fulfillment we must have a citizenship less concerned about what the government can do for it and more anxious about what it can do for the nation.

We drew a pair of deuces and filed.
(on hearing he had won the Republican nomination for president, 1920)

My God, this is a hell of a job! I can take care of my enemies all right. But my damn friends, my God-damn friends. . . . They're the ones that keep me walking the floor nights!

I don't know what to do or where to turn on this taxation matter. Somewhere there must be a book that tells all about it, where I could go to straighten it out in my mind. But I don't know where the book is, and maybe I couldn't read it if I found it! My God, this is a hell of a place for a man like me to be!

Our most dangerous tendency is to expect too much of government, and at the same time do for it too little.

I find a hundred thousand sorrows touching my heart, and there is ringing in my ears like an admonition eternal, an insistent call, "It must not be again!"
(on war)

When politicians play the game of politics, they must play gamely, regardless of the umpire.

☆ CALVIN COOLIDGE ☆

30th President

Birth: July 4, 1872   **Death:** January 5, 1933
Term: August 3, 1923–March 3, 1929

THE COOLIDGE PRESIDENCY

- *Revenue acts of 1924 and 1926 sharply reduced taxes on the wealthy*

- *Charles Lindbergh completes the first transatlantic solo flight (1927)*

Vice President Coolidge was asleep at his father's phoneless farm in Vermont when messengers arrived in the middle of the night with the word that President Harding had died. Coolidge rose, dressed in his best black suit, and took the oath of office on the family Bible, in the presence of his notary-public father and a few witnesses. Then he went back to bed.

Coolidge was born on July 4, 1872, in Plymouth, Vermont, in the family home adjoining his father's general store. He was an average student until his last two years at Amherst College when he excelled, especially in the arts and social sciences. A bit of a loner on campus (Coolidge did not participate in sports or extra-curricular activities), he developed an interest in public service. After graduation, Coolidge studied law with a firm in Northampton, Massachusetts, and was admitted to the bar in 1897.

Although the bride's mother tried her best to prevent their marriage, Coolidge, thirty-three, and Grace Anna Goodhue, twenty-six, married in 1905. Coolidge never reconciled with his mother-in-law, who, for the rest of her life, insisted that Coolidge's political success was due solely to her daughter's skills, efforts, and influence. Although raised a Democrat, Mrs. Coolidge adopted her husband's party. As First Lady she was a popular hostess who obeyed the prohibition law, seeing that no alcohol was served at the White House. The Coolidges were a close and devoted couple although they never discussed matters of state.

Coolidge was not your typical, back-slapping politician. In fact, his main characteristic—keeping his mouth shut—earned him the nickname "Silent Cal." When he made speeches they were short and to the point. Once, at a White House dinner, a young lady sitting next to him said, "Mr. President, I have made a bet I can get more than three words out of you during this meal." Without hesitation, he replied, "You lose."

Coolidge served on the Northampton City Council, as Northampton's city solicitor, and as Hampshire County clerk of courts, prior to being named chairman of the local Republican party. He then held numerous offices, including mayor of Northampton, Massachusetts state senator, lieutenant governor, and governor of Massachusetts.

While he was governor of Massachusetts, the Boston police went on strike. Coolidge promptly called out the entire National Guard and broke the strike, saying, "There is no right to strike against the public safety by anybody, anywhere, at any time." Largely because of this popular action, Coolidge was nominated by the Republicans for vice president in 1920.

On ascending to the presidency upon Harding's death, Coolidge successfully cleaned up the scandals and extravagances of the Harding administration while also reducing the national debt. Coolidge was soon tremendously popular. The country was prosperous and at peace. The voting public felt safe and content. Running on the slogan "Keep Cool with Coolidge," he was easily reelected in 1924. However, there was little joy in the White House. Early in the campaign, the Coolidges' sixteen-year-old son, Calvin, Jr., died of blood poisoning. Devastated, Coolidge said of his son's death:

When he went, the power and the glory of the presidency went with him.

Coolidge chose not to run for reelection in 1928. In typical Coolidge style, he offered no explanation, just the statement "I do not choose to run." In retirement, he returned to Northampton where he wrote his autobiography, various articles, and for a year, a daily newspaper column. He died on January 5, 1933. Shortly before his death, when the Depression was at its deepest, with families ruined and homes lost, he noted, "I no longer fit in with these times."

His last will and testament—in the ultimate Coolidge style—was just twenty-three words in length:

Not unmindful of my son John, I give all my estate, both real and personal, to my wife, Grace Coolidge, in fee simple.

☆ ☆ ☆

I think the American public wants a solemn ass as President and I think I'll go along with them.

There is no dignity quite so impressive, and no independence quite so important, as living within your means.

No person was ever honored for what he received. Honor has been the reward for what he gave.

The business of America is business.

If you don't say anything, you won't be called on to repeat it.

The nation which forgets its defenders will itself be forgotten.
(on the military)

Perhaps one of the most important accomplishments of my administration has been minding my own business.

The President gets the best advice he can find, uses the best judgment at his command, and leaves the event in the hands of Providence.

This country would not be a land of opportunity, America would not be America, if the people were shackled with government monopolies.

You have to stand every day three or four hours of visitors. Nine-tenths of them want something they ought not to have. If you keep dead-still they will run down in three or four minutes. If you even cough or smile they will start up all over again.
(on office seekers)

No nation ever had an army large enough to guarantee it against attack in time of peace, or insure it victory in time of war.

Character is the only secure foundation of the state.

Nothing is easier than spending the public money. It does not appear to belong to anybody.

It is a great advantage to a President, and a major source of safety to the country, for him to know that he is not a great man.

It is the duty of a citizen not only to observe the law but to let it be known that he is opposed to its violation.

Civilization and profits go hand in hand.

There is no right to strike against the public safety by anybody, anywhere, any time.
(*on the Boston police strike of 1919*)

When a great many people are unable to find work, unemployment results.

The President has tended to become the champion of the people because he is held solely responsible for his acts, while in the Congress where responsibility is divided it has developed that there is much greater danger of arbitrary action.

The more I study it [the Constitution] the more I have come to admire it, realizing that no other document devised by the hand of man ever brought so much progress and happiness to humanity.

I shall always consider it the highest tribute to my administration that the opposition have based so little of their criticism on what I have really said and done.

Perhaps one of the reasons I have been a target for so little abuse is because I have tried to refrain from abusing other people.

There is no force so democratic as the force of an ideal.

I've noticed that nothing I've never said has hurt me.

Men speak of natural rights, but I challenge any one to show where in nature any rights existed or were recognized until there was established for their declaration and protection a duly promulgated body of corresponding laws.

The governments of the past could fairly be characterized as devices for maintaining in perpetuity the place and position of certain privileged classes, without any ultimate protection for the rights of the people. The Government of the United States is a device for maintaining in perpetuity the rights of the people, with the ultimate extinction of all privileged classes.

Of course, almost every Democrat thinks the sovereign remedy for any of our ills is the appropriation of public money.

Do the day's work. If it be to protect the rights of the weak, whoever objects, do it. If it be to help a powerful corporation better to serve the people, whatever the opposition, do that.

That man has offered me unsolicited advice for six years, all of it bad.
(on Herbert Hoover)

It is only when men begin to worship that they begin to grow.

Don't expect to build up the weak by pulling down the strong.

Four-fifths of all our troubles in this life would disappear if we would only sit down and keep still.

☆ HERBERT CLARK HOOVER ☆

31st President

Birth: August 10, 1874   Death: October 20, 1964
Term: March 4, 1929–March 3, 1933

THE HOOVER PRESIDENCY

- *Stock market crash (1929)*
- *Great Depression begins (1929)*
- *Empire State Building opens (1931)*

Herbert Hoover went from rags (orphaned at nine) to riches (millionaire by forty); while during his presidency, the nation went from riches to rags (the Great Depression).

Hoover was the first president born west of the Mississippi River, in West Branch, Iowa, on August 10, 1874. At two, Hoover nearly died of the croup. His vital signs imperceptible to his parents, they gave him up for dead, placing pennies on his eyelids and drawing a sheet over his face. Fortunately, his uncle, Dr. John Minthorn, arrived in time to revive him. Hoover was six when his blacksmith father died and nine when his Quaker-minister mother passed away. The three Hoover orphans (Herbert, his brother, and his sister) were divided among relatives. Herbert first went to his Uncle Allan Hoover, then a year later to the physician uncle who had saved his life eight years earlier. An average student, Hoover eventually studied engineering at Stanford, graduating in 1895.

Hoover's first employment after college was as a laborer in a gold mine, where he pushed ore carts for seventy hours a week. Soon, though, his remarkable career started. After securing an office job in San Francisco, he was transferred to Australia where he evaluated the quality of mines about to be purchased. He was then sent to China to develop vast coal deposits. Hoover returned to Australia in 1902, founded his own engineering firm in 1908, and made much of his fortune mining silver in Burma. By 1914, the orphan and ex-laborer was worth $4 million.

In 1899, Hoover, twenty-four, married a Stanford classmate, Lou Henry, also twenty-four. Soon after their marriage, they sailed together to China and Hoover's new job. Mrs. Hoover became quite proficient in Chinese. In fact, at the White House the Hoovers sometimes conversed in Chinese to foil eavesdroppers.

During World War I Hoover gained international attention for his highly efficient distribution of food and supplies to war-ravaged Europe. In 1914 he headed the American Relief Committee which assisted the 120,000 Americans stranded in Europe at the outbreak of war. He then headed the Commission for the Relief of Belgium (1914–19) and the American Relief Administration (1919–20). Simultaneously he served as United States food administrator (1917–18), on the War Trade Council (1917–20), the Sugar Equalization Board (1918–19), the European Coal Council (1919), and as economic advisor to President Wilson at the Versailles Peace Conference. After peace was secured, Hoover served as secretary of commerce for President Harding.

When Coolidge decided not to run again in 1928, Hoover aggressively pursued and secured the Republican presidential nomination. In this, his first election, he bested his Democratic opponent, Alfred E. Smith. Much of the election focused on the issue that Smith was the first Roman Catholic to be nominated for president by a major party. Scurrilous pamphlets distributed without Hoover's knowledge fed the fear that, as president, Smith would annul Protestant marriages and make Catholicism the state religion. The campaign was ugly but effective.

Just months after Hoover took office, the stock market crashed and the Great Depression began. Hoover was cautious and slow to act, for he firmly believed that government should not interfere

with business and that any aid—food or unemployment pay—
should occur at the local level.

The public placed the blame for the horrific economic situation upon Hoover. Those who lost their homes lived in vill-
ages of makeshift shacks called "Hoovervilles." Old newspapers
were "Hoover blankets"; broken automobiles hauled by mules were
"Hoover wagons"; and empty pockets turned inside out were
"Hoover flags."

Congress and the nation waited for 1932, when they might elect
a new President. Franklin Roosevelt easily defeated Hoover.

Hoover first retired to his home in Palo Alto, California, then
spent his later years living at the Waldorf-Astoria Hotel in New
York City. He actively spoke out on all issues of state and was
especially critical of the Democratic social agenda. After World
War II, President Truman appointed Hoover coordinator of the
Food Supply for World Famine (1946–47). He also headed the
Hoover Commission (1953–55), which made hundreds of recommendations for streamlining government. Shortly before his death
on October 20, 1964, Hoover endorsed Barry Goldwater for
president.

☆ ☆ ☆

We in America today are nearer to the final triumph over poverty
than ever before in the history of any land. The poorhouse is van-
ishing from among us. We have not yet reached the goal but given
a chance to go forward with the policies of the last eight years,
and we shall soon, with the help of God, be in sight of the day
when poverty shall be banished from this nation.
(accepting the Republican presidential nomination)

Prosperity cannot be restored by raids upon the public treasury.

It has but few compensations and of them we must make the most. Its greatest compensation lies in the possibility that we may instill into our people unselfishness.
(on war)

The sole function of Government is to bring about a condition of affairs favorable to the beneficial development of private enterprise.

It is a paradox that every dictator has climbed to power on the ladder of free speech. Immediately on attaining power each dictator has suppressed all free speech except his own.

It is a handicap to any man to succeed a member of his own party as President. He has little patronage with which to reward his supporters.

Thank God, she doesn't have to be confirmed by the Senate.
(on hearing of the birth of his granddaughter)

There are only two occasions when Americans respect privacy especially in Presidents. Those are prayer and fishing.

The course of unbalanced budgets is the road to ruin.

Our federal machinery is the result of a hundred years of patchwork and has lagged lamentably behind the skill in organization of our people.
(on bureaucracy)

Commercial business requires a concentration of responsibility. Self-government requires decentralization and many checks and balances to safeguard liberty. Our Government to succeed in business would need to become in effect a despotism. There at once begins the destruction of self-government.

Our country has become the land of opportunity to those born without inheritance, not merely because of the wealth of its resources and industry but because of this freedom of initiative and enterprise.

Free speech does not live many hours after free industry and free commerce die.

Two cars in every garage.

We do not need to burn down the house to kill the rats.

Nobody will deny that the majority of the Congress have been reduced to a rubber stamp for the Executive. They don't deny it themselves.

Many years ago I concluded that a few hair shirts were part of the mental wardrobe of every man. The President differs only from other men in that he has a more extensive wardrobe.

Presidents have long since learned that one of the undisclosed articles in the Bill of Rights is that criticism and digging of political graves are reserved exclusively to members of the legislative arm.

Children are our most valuable natural resource.

When there is a lack of honor in government, the morals of the whole people are poisoned.

Older men declare war. But it is youth that must fight and die. And it is youth who must inherit the tribulation, the sorrow, and the triumphs that are the aftermath of war.

Every time the government is forced to act, we lose something in self-reliance, character and initiative.

Once upon a time my political opponents honored me as possessing the fabulous intellectual and economic power by which I created a world-wide depression all by myself.

No man can be just a little crooked.

The worst evil of disregard for some law is that it destroys respect for all law.

The reconstruction of children is more precious than factories and bridges.

True Liberalism is found not in striving to spread bureaucracy but in striving to set bounds to it.

Progress of the nation is the sum of progress of its individuals.

I outlived the bastards.
(on those that blamed him for the Depression)

Franklin Delano
☆ Roosevelt ☆

32nd President

Birth: January 30, 1882   Death: April 12, 1945
Term: March 4, 1933–April 12, 1945

THE ROOSEVELT (FRANKLIN) PRESIDENCY

- *Repeal of Prohibition (Twenty-first Amendment, 1933)*
- *Tennessee Valley Authority (TVA), Civilian Conservation Corps (CCC), Public Works Administration (PWA), and National Recovery Administration (NRA) created (1933)*
- *Social Security Act passed (1935)*
- *National minimum wage enacted (1938)*
- *World War II begins (1939)*
- *United States enters war (1941)*
- *Churchill, Stalin, and Roosevelt confer at Yalta (1945)*

Franklin Delano Roosevelt was quite the family man:

- he was the seventh cousin, once removed, of Winston Churchill;
- his mother was the sixth cousin of his father;
- he was related to eleven other presidents: Theodore Roosevelt (fifth cousin), Washington, both Adamses, Madison, Van Buren, both Harrisons, Taylor (fourth cousin three times removed), Grant, and Taft; and
- he married his fifth cousin, once removed, Eleanor Roosevelt.

Born on January 30, 1882, Franklin Roosevelt did not arrive easily—his delivery nearly killed both mother and child. After long hours of unsuccessful labor, the attending physician administered an overdose of chloroform to his mother. She turned blue and passed out. Then Franklin was born, also blue and unconscious. Only mouth-to-mouth resuscitation breathed life into the future president.

Roosevelt had a happy and privileged childhood (he had his own pony, and at age sixteen, his own sailboat), enjoying himself with his family at their summer home on Campobello Island and on trips abroad.

Roosevelt received his early education from a series of tutors and attended Groton, Harvard, and Columbia Law School. An average student, he considered the highlight of his collegiate career to be his tenure as editor of the Harvard *Crimson*. Although he never finished law school, he was admitted to the bar in 1907 and joined a New York City law firm.

On March 17, 1905, Roosevelt (Franklin) and Roosevelt (Eleanor) married. When President Theodore Roosevelt was asked what he thought of his niece's marriage to her fifth cousin, once removed, he replied, "It is a good thing to keep the name in the family." When Franklin was stricken with polio in 1921, Eleanor nursed and prodded him back to an active life. She had to overcome her shyness to make public appearances on his behalf. Thereafter, throughout their marriage and his political career, she served as his representative. She was thus the first First Lady to be actively involved in matters of substance. In 1918, Eleanor learned that her husband was having an affair with Lucy Page Mercer. Eleanor demanded that the relationship end, threatening FDR with divorce. He ended the relationship, but resumed it later, with Lucy often visiting the White House while Eleanor traveled. Lucy was even with the President when he was fatally stricken with a cerebral hemorrhage in Warm Springs, Georgia (Lucy was quickly hustled away before Eleanor arrived).

Roosevelt began his political career in the New York State Senate (1911–13). He then served as assistant secretary of the navy (1913–20), and was defeated in a 1914 campaign for the U.S. Senate. In 1920 he ran as the vice presidential nominee on the Democratic ticket with James M. Cox (they lost to Harding and Coolidge).

A year later, having returned to private law practice, Roosevelt was stricken with polio. After three painful and persistent years of convalescence, he returned to the political arena, nominating Alfred E. Smith for president in 1924 and again in 1928. He served as governor of New York from 1929 to 1933 and announced his candidacy for the presidency in January 1932.

With the theme song "Happy Days Are Here Again," and the slogan "Kick Out Depression with a Democratic Vote," Roosevelt embarked upon a strenuous campaign travel schedule to erase any doubts about an invalid serving as president. He trounced an exhausted Hoover haunted by the Great Depression. In his reelection of 1936, Roosevelt overwhelmed Alf M. Landon (Landon carried only two states). Roosevelt was reelected again in 1940 (defeating Wendell Willkie) with the pledge to keep the United States out of World War II while continuing the policies of his New Deal. In 1944, with Senator Harry Truman as his running mate, Roosevelt hid his failing health and again won reelection. During this campaign, Roosevelt's last, a united public voted not to change leadership in the midst of a war, especially when the current president's opponent, Thomas E. Dewey, lacked foreign-policy experience.

Roosevelt's long presidency was dominated by World War II and the New Deal. Confronted with the worst economic depression in the country's history, Roosevelt launched the New Deal, a massive program of direct federal relief and economic regulation. It included, among many other efforts, the establishment of the Civilian Conservation Corps, which hired the young and poor to build roads and work on conservation projects; the Tennessee Valley Authority, which aided the depressed Tennessee Valley by harnessing floodwaters for conversion to electricity; the Federal Emergency Relief Administration, which provided assistance to the poor; the Works Progress Administration, which provided useful employment requiring a wide range of skills, from bricklaying to acting; the Rural Electrification Administration, which funded the extension of electrical power into rural areas; and the National Industrial Recovery Act, which provided funds to states and cities for large construction projects.

To marshal wide support for these efforts, Roosevelt spoke directly over the radio to "the people." In these talks, which would become known as "fireside chats," the president's warm and vibrant voice calmly reassured a once-confident nation stunned by a seemingly endless and hopeless depression.

In 1933, the first woman Cabinet member in the nation's history joined Roosevelt's administration. Frances Perkins, who served as secretary of labor until 1945, was instrumental in the establishment of the Social Security system in 1935 and passage of the Fair Labor Standards Act of 1938.

Throughout 1940 and 1941, the United States edged closer and closer to participation in the war in Germany. Then on December 7, 1941, the Japanese bombed Pearl Harbor in Hawaii, killing 2,300 Americans and destroying much of the United States Pacific fleet. Claiming that the date of the attack "will live in infamy," Roosevelt asked Congress the very next day for a declaration of war. He declared:

Hostilities exist. There is no blinking at the fact that our people, our territory, and our interests are in grave danger.

Displaying the same spirit with which he faced polio and the Depression, Roosevelt led the nation in a massive and successful war effort. With the end of the war in sight, Roosevelt met with Churchill and Soviet Premier Josef Stalin at Yalta in February 1945. In return for a Soviet pledge to enter the war against Japan after Germany's surrender, Stalin was granted certain concessions that would strengthen the Soviet hand in the years following the war.

On April 12, 1945, just when Roosevelt was about to see the horrible war brought to an end on both the European and Pacific fronts, and while an artist was sketching his portrait, he suddenly pressed his hand to his forehead and cried out, "I have a terrific headache."

Those would be his last words. He died two and a half hours later.

These economic royalists complain that we seek to overthrow the institutions of America. What they really complain of is that we seek to take away their power. These economic royalists are unanimous in their hate for me—and I welcome their hatred.

I have no expectation of making a hit every time I come to bat. What I seek is the highest possible batting average.

A conservative is a man with two perfectly good legs, who, however, has never learned to walk.

One thing is sure. We have to do something. We have to do the best we know how at the moment. If it doesn't turn out right, we can modify it as we go along.

The test of our progress is not whether we add more to the abundance of those who have much; it is whether we provide enough for those who have little.

There is a mysterious cycle in human events. To some generations much is given. Of other generations much is expected. This generation of Americans has a rendezvous with destiny.

We are fighting to save a great and precious form of government for ourselves and for the world.
(on World War II)

These unhappy times call for the building of plans . . . that build from the bottom up and not from the top down, that put their faith once more in the forgotten man at the bottom of the economic pyramid.

There are many ways it can be helped, but it can never be helped by merely talking about it. We must act, and we must act quickly.
(on the Depression)

The country needs and, unless I mistake its temper, the country demands bold, persistent experimentation. It is common sense to take a method and try it; if it fails, admit it frankly and try another. But above all, try something.

Be sincere; be brief; be seated.
(on speechmaking)

The overwhelming majority of Americans are possessed of two great qualities—a sense of humor and a sense of proportion.

We must especially be aware of that small group of selfish men who would clip the wings of the American eagle in order to feather their own nests.

We . . . would rather die on our feet than live on our knees.

For three long years I have been going up and down this country preaching that government . . . costs too much. I shall not stop that preaching.

We can afford all that we need; but we cannot afford all that we want.

If we do not halt this steady process of building commissions and regulatory bodies and special legislation like huge inverted pyramids over every one of the simple constitutional provisions, we shall soon be spending many billions of dollars more.
(on bureaucracy)

The royalists of the economic order have conceded that political freedom was the business of government, but they have maintained that economic slavery was nobody's business.

Concentration of wealth and power has been built upon other people's money, other people's business, other people's labor. Under this concentration, independent business . . . has been a menace to . . . American society.

Private enterprise is ceasing to be free enterprise.

I pledge you, I pledge myself, to a new deal for the American people.

I consider it a public duty to answer falsifications with facts. I will not pretend that I find this an unpleasant duty. I am an old campaigner, and I love a good fight.

I want to go back to Hyde Park. I want to take care of my trees. I want to make the farm pay. I want to finish my little house on the hill.

Since the beginning of our American history we have been engaged in change—in a perpetual peaceful revolution—a revolution which goes on steadily, quietly adjusting itself to changing conditions—without the concentration camp or the quicklime in the ditch.

Yesterday, December 7, 1941—a date which will live in infamy— the United States of America was suddenly and deliberately attacked by naval and air forces of the Empire of Japan.

The United States Constitution has proved itself the most marvelously elastic compilation of rules of government ever written.

Our Constitution is so simple and practical that it is possible always to meet extraordinary needs by changes in emphasis and arrangement without loss of essential form.

These Republican leaders have not been content with attacks upon me, or on my wife, or on my sons—no, not content with that, they now include my little dog, Fala. Unlike the members of my family, he resents this.

Any government, like any family, can for a year spend a little more than it earns. But you and I know that a continuance of that habit means the poorhouse.

Let us have the courage to stop borrowing to meet continuing deficits. Stop the deficits.

Not only our future economic soundness but the very soundness of our democratic institutions depends on the determination of our government to give employment to idle men. The people of America are in agreement in defending their liberties at any cost, and the first line of defense lies in the protection of economic security.

The ablest man I ever met is the man you think you are.

Let me assert my firm belief that the only thing we have to fear is fear itself—nameless, unreasoning, unjustified terror which paralyzes needed efforts to convert retreat into advance.

We look forward to a world founded upon four essential human freedoms. The first is freedom of speech and expression everywhere in the world. The second is freedom of every person to worship God in his own way everywhere in the world. The third is freedom from want . . . everywhere in the world. The fourth is freedom from fear . . . anywhere in the world.

To stand upon the ramparts and die for our principles is heroic, but to sally forth to battle and win for our principles is something more than heroic.

No man can tame a tiger by stroking it.

We are now in the midst of a war, not for conquest, not for vengeance, but for a world in which this nation, and all that this nation represents, will be safe for our children. . . . We are going to win the war and we are going to win the peace that follows.

Never before have we had so little time in which to do so much.

The only limit to our realization of tomorrow will be our doubts of today.

No business which depends for its existence on paying less than living wages to its workers has any right to continue in this country.

It's a terrible thing to look over your shoulder when you are trying to lead—and find no one there.

Those who would give up essential liberty to purchase a little temporary safety deserve neither liberty nor safety.

A government can be no better than the public opinion that sustains it.

☆ HARRY S TRUMAN ☆

33rd President

Birth: May 8, 1884   Death: December 26, 1972
Term: April 12, 1945–January 20, 1953

THE TRUMAN PRESIDENCY

- *Atomic bombs dropped on Japan (1945)*
- *World War II ends (1945)*
- *United Nations charter signed (1945)*
- *Nuremberg Trials (1945–46)*
- *Creation of Israel (1948)*
- *NATO Treaty authorized (1949)*
- *Korean War (1950–53)*
- *Twenty-second Amendment ratified ("no person shall be elected to the office of the President more than twice," 1951)*
- *Puerto Rico became a United States Commonwealth (1952)*

Harry S Truman's mother, Martha Ellen Young Truman, was the daughter of a Confederate family that was briefly locked up in a federal "internment camp" during the Civil War. For this, Mrs. Truman never fully forgave President Lincoln or the federal government. Once, when offered certain accommodations at the White House, she refused, saying she'd rather sleep on the floor "than spend the night in the Lincoln bed."

Harry S Truman was born in the family home in Lamar, Missouri. The "S" in his name is not an abbreviation but his complete middle name, the result of a parental compromise between naming

176

him after his paternal grandfather (Anderson Shippe Truman) or his maternal grandfather (Solomon Young). A boy of slight build with eyeglasses, Truman grew up on farms near Harrisonville and Grandview before the family settled in Independence, Missouri. Truman claimed that as a boy

> I was never popular. . . . Without my glasses I was blind as a bat, and to tell the truth, I was kind of a sissy.

But he was a voracious reader, having borrowed every book in the town library by the age of fourteen. His early heroes included Hannibal and Robert E. Lee; he disdained Alexander the Great and Napoleon because he felt they fought for conquest and not principle.

Truman, an average student, hoped to attend West Point, but his poor eyesight made that an impossibility. An accomplished pianist, he once fancied a musical career, but when his father went broke in 1901—the year of Truman's high-school graduation—such hopes were dropped in favor of work. His professional life over the next twenty years was, at best, checkered. He was a timekeeper, mailroom clerk, bank clerk, bookkeeper, farmer, soldier (World War I), a failed investor, and a bankrupt haberdasher.

He eventually turned to politics, first serving as a judge in Jackson County (Missouri), an administrative post similar to county executive. During this time he attended law school, led the Democratic party for the county's Eastern District, served as president of the Greater Kansas City Plan Association, directed the National Conference on City Planning, and headed up the Federal Emergency Relief Administration. He then served as U.S. Senator (1935–45) and vice president from March to April of 1945.

Truman, thirty-five, and Elizabeth "Bess" Virginia Wallace, thirty-four, married on June 28, 1919. They first met in Sunday school when he was six and she five. From then on, apparently, Harry was in love. Bess, however, resented Truman's decision to accept the vice presidency and went on to hate her years in the White House. According to their only child, Margaret, an "emotional separation" developed between the president and First Lady. Mrs. Truman discontinued the First Lady press conferences initiated by Eleanor Roosevelt, and official entertainment during the Truman years was quite limited. Mrs. Truman was the longest-lived First Lady, dying on October 18, 1982, at the age of ninety-seven.

Truman ascended to the presidency on April 12, 1945, upon the death of President Roosevelt. When told by Eleanor Roosevelt that the president was dead, Truman asked, "Is there anything I can do for you?" She replied, "Is there anything *we* can do for *you*? For you are the one in trouble now." The next day he told a gathering of reporters, "Boys, if you ever pray, pray for me now."

Within a month of his taking office, the war in Europe came to an end and Truman traveled to Europe to help draw up the peace. He then faced the decision of whether to use the atomic bomb on Japan. He chose to; and the war in the Pacific also ended.

Truman now faced a multitude of postwar problems. Much of Europe lay in ruins. Millions were homeless and starving. America began to pour massive aid into the war-torn countries.

In the election of 1948 against Thomas E. Dewey, governor of New York, most everyone dismissed Truman as a mere caretaker president doomed to defeat . . . everyone except Harry Truman. Truman traveled back and forth across the country, making more than 350 speeches. To his delight and the embarrassment of the many newspapers and pollsters who had confidently predicted his overwhelming defeat, Truman won.

After his reelection, he continued to face a multitude of postwar challenges. He approved Secretary of State George Marshall's European Recovery Program (the Marshall Plan) to rebuild Europe with some $13 billion of reconstruction projects. In March 1947, Truman stated:

I believe that it must be the policy of the United States to support free peoples who are resisting attempted subjugation by armed minorities or by outside pressures.

This was the heart of the Truman Doctrine, an effort not to liberate countries already in the grip of communism but rather to check its spread—a policy of containment.

The Korean War began during Truman's presidency in June 1950, when North Korean Communist forces invaded South Korea. Truman secured a United Nations mandate to expel the North Koreans with a United Nations force under the popular World War II hero, General Douglas MacArthur's command. When these forces, 90 percent of whom were American or South Korean, were defeated by the forces of Red China, MacArthur insisted that Truman declare war on China. When Truman refused, the general publicly refuted his commander in chief, provoking Truman to fire him.

Truman's domestic policy, popularly known as the Fair Deal, provided federal funds for slum clearance and urban renewal, an increase in the minimum wage, extension of Social Security coverage, and desegregation of the armed forces.

Communism was fought not just in Asia but throughout the streets and corridors of the nation's capital. The McCarran Internal Security Act of 1950—passed over Truman's veto—required Communists in the United States to register with the Justice Department and restricted their activities. Sensational espionage trials suggested that Washington was thick with traitors. In 1950, Republican Senator Joseph McCarthy claimed to have a list of 205 names of known Communists in the State Department. Although he failed to produce one shred of evidence to back up the charge, he rose to prominence on the issue, denouncing the Roosevelt and Truman administrations for "twenty years of treason."

In 1951, the Twenty-second Amendment to the Constitution

was ratified, limiting future presidents to two terms in office. Although Truman was eligible to run again, he instead retired to Independence, Missouri, where for the next twenty years he actively supported candidates in both local and national elections. His health had been failing for several years when he fell unconscious on Christmas, 1972. The next day he died.

Three things ruin a man. Power, money, and women. I never wanted power. I never had any money, and the only woman in my life is up at the house right now.

Being too good is apt to be uninteresting.

Whenever you have an efficient government you have a dictatorship.

The trouble with Eisenhower is he's just a coward. He hasn't got any backbone at all.

I learned that a leader is a man who has the ability to get other people to do what they don't want to do, and like it.

Being a President is like riding a tiger. A man has to keep on riding or be swallowed. The fantastically crowded months of 1945 taught me that a President either is constantly on top of events, or, if he hesitates, events will soon be on top of him. I never felt that I could let up for a moment.

In the middle of the speech, some big voice up in the corner hollered out, "Give 'em hell, Harry!" Well, I never gave anybody hell—I just told the truth on these fellows and they thought it was hell.

It is hot and humid and lonely. Why in hell does anybody want to be a head of state? Damned if I know.

You know, right here is where I've always wanted to be, and the only place I've ever wanted to be. The Senate—that's just my speed and style.

It's a recession when your neighbor loses his job. It's a depression when you lose yours.

All the President is, is a glorified public-relations man who spends his time flattering, kissing, and kicking people to get them to do what they are supposed to do anyway.

I fired MacArthur because he wouldn't respect the authority of the President. I didn't fire him because he was a dumb son of a bitch, although he was, but that's not against the law for generals. If it was, half to three-quarters of them would be in jail.

Slanders, lies, character assassination—these things are a threat to every single citizen everywhere in this country. When even one American—who has done nothing wrong—is forced by fear to shut his mind and close his mouth—then all Americans are in peril. It is the job of every American who loves his country and his freedom—to rise up and put a stop to this terrible business.

The Presidency is an all-day and nearly an all-night job. Just between you and me and the gatepost, I like it.

Nixon is a shifty-eyed goddamn liar, and people know it. He's one of the few in the history of this country to run for high office talking out of both sides of his mouth at the same time and lying out of both sides.

There is an epitaph in Boot Hill Cemetery in Arizona which reads: "Here lies Jack Williams. He done his damnedest!" What more can a person do? Well, that's all I could do. I did my damnedest, and that's all there is to it.

John Adams and Thomas Jefferson were political enemies, but they became fast friends. And when they passed away on the same day, the last words of one of them was, "The country is safe. Jefferson still lives." And the last words of the other was, "John Adams will see that things go forward."

The President cannot function without advisers or without advice, written or oral. But just as soon as he is required to show what kind of advice he has had, who said what to him, or what kind of records he has, the advice received will be worthless.

I have had enough experience in all my years, and have read enough of the past, to know that advice to grandchildren is usually wasted. If the second and third generations could profit by the experience of the first generation, we would not be having some of the troubles we have today.

As you get older, you get tired of doing the same things over and over again, so you think Christmas has changed. It hasn't. It's you who has changed.

America was not built on fear. America was built on courage, on imagination and unbeatable determination to do the job at hand.

You know that being an American is more than a matter of where your parents came from. It is a belief that all men are created free and equal and that everyone deserves an even break. It is respect for the dignity of men and women without regard to race, creed, or color. That is our creed.

Sixteen hours ago an American airplane dropped one bomb on Hiroshima . . . The force from which the sun draws its powers has been loosed against those who brought the war in the Far East. *(August 6, 1945)*

If a [decision to drop the atomic bomb] had to be made for the welfare of the United States and the democracies of the world, I wouldn't hesitate to make it again.

It is part of my responsibility as Commander-in-Chief of the armed forces to see to it that our country is able to defend itself against any possible aggressor. Accordingly, I have directed the Atomic Energy Commission to continue its work on all forms of atomic weapons, including the so-called hydrogen or super-bomb.

The atomic bomb was no "great decision." . . . It was merely another powerful weapon in the arsenal of righteousness.

I'm going to fight hard. I'm going to give them hell.

A President has to expect those things. The only thing you have to worry about is bad luck. I never have bad luck. *(after assassination attempt at Blair House, November 1, 1950)*

We can take heart from a comment made by that great American heavyweight champion Joe Lewis. In one fight, some time ago, he had a hard time catching up with his opponent. But Joe finally did catch up with him, and he knocked him out. After the fight, this is what Joe said: "Well, he could run away, but he couldn't hide."

It isn't important who is ahead at one time or another in either an election or a horse race. It's the horse that comes in first at the finish that counts.

A man cannot have character unless he lives within a fundamental system of morals that creates character.

The menace of communism lies primarily in those areas of American life where the promise of democracy remains unfulfilled.

But the great danger of communism does not lie in its false promises. It lies in the fact that it is an instrument of an armed imperialism which seeks to extend its influence by force.

If you tell Congress everything about the world situation, they get hysterical. If you tell them nothing, they go fishing.

If there is one basic element in our Constitution, it is civilian control of the military.

When they told me yesterday what had happened, I felt like the moon, the stars and all the planets had fallen on me.
(to reporters, the day after his accession to the presidency)

Study men, not historians.

Men make history and not the other way around. In periods where there is no leadership, society stands still. Progress occurs when courageous, skillful leaders seize the opportunity to change things for the better.

If you can't convince them, confuse them.

The buck stops here.
(sign on Truman's desk)

Most of the problems a President has to face have their roots in the past.

If you can't stand the heat, get out of the kitchen.

Everybody is headed for the same place, and they are headed on the same train, and under the same engineer.

I never sit on a fence. I am either on one side or another.

You don't set a fox to watching the chickens just because he has a lot of experience in the hen house.
(on Richard Nixon's candidacy, 1960)

The Marine Corps . . . today have a propaganda machine that is almost equal to Stalin's.

It was said in the First World War that the French fought for their country, the British fought for freedom of the seas, and the Americans fought for souvenirs.

In the simplest terms, what we are doing in Korea is this: We are trying to prevent a third world war.

Our goal must not be peace in our time, but peace for all time.

☆ DWIGHT DAVID EISENHOWER ☆

34th President

Birth: October 14, 1890   Death: March 28, 1969
Term: January 20, 1953–January 20, 1961

THE EISENHOWER PRESIDENCY

- *Korean War ends (1953)*
- *Supreme Court declares racial segregation in schools unconstitutional (1954)*
- *Construction of Interstate Highway System authorized (1956)*
- *Federal troops sent to Little Rock, Arkansas, to enforce integration (1957)*
- *NASA (National Aeronautics and Space Administration) established (1958)*
- *Alaska and Hawaii admitted as forty-ninth and fiftieth states (1959)*
- *St. Lawrence Seaway opened (1959)*

The mother of Dwight D. Eisenhower, the great World War II general who led the Allied forces to victory in Europe, was a devout pacifist. When she found her young son reading about battles and heroes (his favorites were Hannibal and George Washington), she took the books and locked them in the attic. Years later, when she put the future military hero on the train to West Point, she went home and wept. It was the first time her family had ever seen her cry.

Eisenhower—known as "Ike"—was born in a rented room near the railroad tracks in Denison, Texas. While he was still an infant, the family moved to Abilene, Kansas. After Ike's father went bankrupt, the Eisenhowers found themselves in severe poverty. Ike and his brothers, who wore hand-me-downs, including their mother's shoes, refused to be teased by those better off. Instead, they were quick to settle a score with their fists (at which they almost always succeeded). Ike was an average student and a very good athlete. At West Point, he graduated sixty-first in a class of 164 and was well on his way to being a collegiate football star when he seriously injured his knee.

On graduation from West Point in 1915, Eisenhower was commissioned a second lieutenant. His military career included service in Texas, Georgia, Maryland, Pennsylvania, New Jersey, back to Georgia, Panama, Kansas, Washington, the Philippines, Washington (again), and back to Texas. By 1941, he was a colonel.

On July 1, 1916, Eisenhower, twenty-five, married Marie "Mamie" Geneva Doud, nineteen. The daughter of a prosperous meat packer, Mamie was accustomed to more creature comforts than those afforded at military posts. However, she adjusted readily and joined her husband in moving twenty-eight times before their retirement at the end of his presidency. Mamie suffered from Ménière's disease, a disorder of the inner ear that often left her dizzy and off balance. In later years, this condition prompted baseless rumors that Mamie had a drinking problem.

After the Japanese attack on Pearl Harbor, Eisenhower was summoned to Washington to become assistant chief of staff in charge of war plans. After a series of promotions, in December 1943 he was named Supreme Allied Commander with specific orders to mount an invasion of German-controlled Europe. A little more than two years later, on May 7, 1945, he accepted Germany's surrender. In 1948 he resigned from the army. Although horrified by the proven destructive capabilities of the atomic bomb, he was hopeful that it might serve as a deterrent to World War III.

He was appointed president of Columbia University, where he was actively wooed by both political parties to be their presidential candidate in 1948. He declined both. In 1952, however, he agreed to run for the presidency on the Republican ticket. He campaigned extensively but stayed above the daily dirt of politics, leaving personal attacks on Democrats to his running mate, Richard M. Nixon. The simple slogan "I like Ike" proved effective, and Eisenhower won the election over Adlai E. Stevenson. The Eisenhower-Nixon team bested Stevenson again in 1956.

Eisenhower's great hope was that as president he could work for peace. He had seen enough war, he said. As he promised during the campaign, Ike personally went to Korea and concluded a peace treaty. With Cuba going Communist, Senator Joseph McCarthy witch-hunting for government "pinkos," and Vietnam on the brink of a Communist takeover, the cold war was now at its height. Eisenhower's strategy was to deter Soviet aggression by threatening massive retaliation; he launched the arms race by directing a huge buildup of nuclear missiles.

Joseph McCarthy's anti-Communist crusade continued into the Eisenhower administration until 1954. During the Army-McCarthy hearings, convened to investigate charges of Communist infiltration of the Defense Department, McCarthy's tactic of bullying witnesses was exposed during the nationally televised proceedings, and he quickly fell into disgrace.

Also in 1954, in the wake of the Supreme Court's desegregation decision, violence erupted in Little Rock (Arkansas) where black students were attempting to enroll in a previously all-white high school. Eisenhower dispatched federal troops to assure the safety of the students and the enforcement of federal law.

During his presidency, Eisenhower enjoyed using Shangri-la, Franklin Roosevelt's former weekend retreat in the Maryland mountains. However, because it sounded "just a little too fancy for a Kansas farm boy," Eisenhower changed its name from Shangri-la to Camp David (after his grandson, David Eisenhower).

When he left the White House at age seventy (making him, up to that time, the oldest person to hold the office of president), he retired to a farm in Gettysburg, Pennsylvania. Because so much of his life had been spent in the army, his retirement residence was the very first house he and Mrs. Eisenhower had ever owned. In retirement, he wrote, golfed, and, from time to time, backed political candidates—Nixon and Goldwater—and supported various issues—such as the war in Vietnam. After a series of heart attacks between 1965 and 1969 (he had also suffered a heart attack while president in 1955), Eisenhower died on March 28, 1969. His last words were: "I want to go; God take me."

☆ ☆ ☆

I hate war as only a soldier who has lived it can, only as one who has seen its brutality, its futility, its *stupidity*.

Here in America we are descended in blood and in spirit from revolutionaries and rebels—men and women who dared to dissent from accepted doctrine. As their heirs, may we never confuse honest dissent with disloyal subversion.

You know, once in a while I get to the point, with everybody staring at me, where I want to go back indoors and pull down the curtains.

I can think of nothing more boring, for the American public, than to have to sit in their living rooms for a whole half an hour looking at my face on their television screens.

There's only one man who has seen more of the world and talked with more people and knows more than he [John Foster Dulles] does—and that's me.

Accomplishment will prove to be a journey, not a destination.

Farming looks mighty easy when your plow is a pencil and you're a thousand miles from a cornfield.

We cannot live alone, and we've got to find some way for our allies to earn a living, because we do not want to carry them on our backs.

We failed to halt Hirohito, Mussolini and Hitler by not acting in unity and in time. That marked the beginning of many years of stark tragedy and desperate peril. May it not be that our nations have learned something from that lesson?
(*telegram to Churchill, 1954, urging unity in Vietnam*)

No one should be appointed to political office if he is a seeker after it.

The last thing I would ever ask any man that I appoint to a high office is what are going to be his decisions in specific cases.

Patronage is almost a wicked word. By itself it could well-nigh defeat democracy.

The necessary and wise subordination of the military to civil power will be best sustained when lifelong professional soldiers abstain from seeking high political office.

In the council of government we must guard against the acquisition of unwanted influence, whether sought or unsought, by the military-industrial complex . . . We must never let the weight of this combination endanger our liberties or democratic processes. We should take nothing for granted. Only an alert and knowledgeable citizenry can compel the proper meshing of the huge industrial and military machinery of defense with our peaceful methods and goals so that security and liberty may prosper together.

The worst to be feared and the best to be expected can be simply stated. The worst is atomic war. The best would be this: a life of perpetual fear and tension; a burden of arms draining the wealth and labor of all peoples. Every gun that is made, every warship launched, every rocket fired, signified, in the final sense, a theft from those who hunger and are not fed, those who are cold and are not clothed.

This titanic force must be reduced to the fruitful service of mankind.
(on the atomic bomb)

It is not enough to take this weapon [the atomic bomb] out of the hands of soldiers. It must be put into the hands of those who will know how to strip its military casing and adapt it to the arts of peace.

But for me to say that the defense capabilities of the United States are such that they could inflict terrible losses upon an aggressor— for me to say that the retaliation capabilities of the United States are such that an aggressor's land would be laid waste—all this, while fact, is not the true expression of the purpose and the hope of the United States. To pause there would be to confirm the hopeless finality of a belief that two atomic colossi are doomed malevolently to eye each other indefinitely across a trembling world.
(arms race)

Destruction is not a good police force.

Look, I'd like to know what's on the other side of the moon. But I won't pay to find out this year!

Whatever America hopes to bring to pass in this world must first come to pass in the heart of America.

Neither a wise man nor a brave man lies down on the tracks of history to wait for the train of the future to run over him.

#

I can't imagine any set of circumstances that would ever induce me to send federal troops into . . . any area to enforce the orders of a federal court, because I believe that [the] common sense of America will never require it.

Mob rule cannot be allowed to override the decisions of our courts.

I deplore the need or the use of troops anywhere to get American citizens to obey the orders of constituted courts; but I want to point this one thing out: there is no person in this room whose basic rights are not involved in any successful defiance to the carrying out of court orders.

I do not see how any American can justify—legally, or logically, or morally—a discrimination in the expenditure of those [federal] funds as among our citizens. If there is any benefit to be derived from them, I think it means all share, regardless of such inconsequential factors as race and religion.

I will use the full power of the United States including whatever force will be necessary to prevent any obstruction of the law and to carry out the orders of the Federal Court.

The standing of the United States as the most powerful of the anticolonial powers is an asset of incalculable value to the free world.

Unless we can put things in the hands of people who are starving to death we can never lick Communism.

We face a hostile ideology—global in scope, atheistic in character, ruthless in purpose, and insidious in method.
(on communism)

The selfishness of the members of Congress is incredible . . . They are just about driving me nuts.

When it comes down to the relations of any President with a Congress controlled by the opposite party, I just say this: it is no bed of roses.

No treaty or international agreement can contravene the Constitution.

Don't join the book burners. Don't think you are going to conceal faults by concealing evidence that they never existed.

An intellectual is a man who takes more words than necessary to tell more than he knows.

Biggest damfool mistake I ever made.
(on his appointment of Earl Warren as chief justice)

I just won't get into a pissing contest with that skunk.
(on Senator Joe McCarthy)

You might have the broader consideration that might follow what you would call the "falling domino" principle. You have a row of dominos set up, you knock over the first one, and what will happen to the last one is the certainty that it will go over very quickly.

Politics should be the part-time profession of every citizen.

In war there is no substitute for victory.

Men acquainted with the battlefield will not be found among the numbers that glibly talk of another war.

More than any other war in history, this war has been an array of the forces of evil against those of righteousness. It had to have its leaders and it had to be won—but no matter what the sacrifice, no matter what the suffering of populations, no matter what the cost, the war had to be won.
(on World War II)

Weakness cannot cooperate with anything. Only strength can cooperate.

I would rather persuade a man to go along, because once he has been persuaded he will stick. If I scare him, he will stay just as long as he is scared, and then he is gone.

The middle of the road is all of the usable surface. The extremes, right and left, are in the gutters.

The quest for peace is the statesman's most exacting duty.

I want to go; God take me.
(his last words)

☆ JOHN FITZGERALD KENNEDY ☆

35th President

Birth: May 29, 1917   Death: November 22, 1963
Term: January 20, 1961–November 22, 1963

THE KENNEDY PRESIDENCY

- *East Germany closes border between East and West Berlin (1961)*
- *Peace Corps created (1961)*
- *Failed Bay of Pigs Invasion (1961)*
- *First United States astronauts explore space (1961–63)*
- *Civil Rights legislation (1961–63)*
- *Cuban Missile Crisis (1962)*
- *Supreme Court declares public-school prayers unconstitutional (1962)*

John F. Kennedy, never a particularly religious Roman Catholic, nonetheless attended confession regularly. Because he worried that a priest might recognize his famous voice and someday reveal his confession, Kennedy would go to church with a group of Catholic Secret Service men and find an inconspicuous place in the middle of the line. On one occasion the ruse failed so miserably that when Kennedy stepped into the booth, the priest said, "Good evening, Mr. President." Kennedy walked out immediately.

"Jack" Kennedy was the first president born in the twentieth century (May 29, 1917, at his family's home in Brookline, Massachusetts). Because his father, Joseph Patrick Kennedy, was an extremely wealthy businessman and diplomat, Kennedy grew up in comfort, living in Brookline and New York City, at the family's summer home on Cape Cod and at their winter quarters in Palm Beach, Florida. He was such a sickly child (he survived whooping cough, tonsillitis, jaundice, measles, chicken pox, scarlet fever, and appendicitis) that his older brother, Joe, used to tease that a mosquito took a big risk in biting Jack. At twenty-one, Jack, like each of his eight siblings, came into a $1 million trust fund. An average student more interested in pranks than scholarship, Jack graduated in 1940 from Harvard where he was on the football, golf, sailing, and swim teams, and an editor of the Harvard *Crimson*.

After graduation he served in World War II. He became a hero when, as the skipper of the *PT-109*, his ship was sunk and he successfully saved the lives of all but two crew members. After his military discharge, he worked as a journalist for a short period before being elected a U.S. congressman from Massachusetts (1947–53). He then served as a U.S. senator (1953–61).

In 1960 he ran for the presidency against Richard M. Nixon, with Lyndon B. Johnson as his running mate (both to secure southern votes and get Johnson out of the Senate where he could harm Kennedy's legislative initiatives). It was initially assumed that the more experienced Nixon would win the election. But televised debates in which Kennedy appeared fresh, fit, and composed while Nixon looked haggard, pale, and menacing, swayed just enough voters to give Kennedy an extremely slim margin of victory.

On September 12, 1953, Kennedy, thirty-six, had married Jacqueline "Jackie" Bouvier, twenty-four. They had a girl and a boy who lived to maturity—Caroline and John—and for the first time in decades, children again played in the White House.

Kennedy's short and popular presidency was marked by social advances and by ongoing tension with the Soviet Union. Kennedy established the Peace Corps to enlist volunteers in teaching and providing technical manpower to underdeveloped countries. His administration responded to black demands for civil rights with executive action, a legislative program, and moral leadership.

Kennedy's hope for more friendly relations with the Soviet Union were dealt a near-fatal blow only months into his presidency when he supported an unsuccessful invasion of Soviet-supported Cuba by anti-Castro Cubans. This failed effort is known as the Bay of Pigs Invasion. It harmed American prestige in Latin America and threatened American-Soviet relations as well. (Immediately after this fiasco, Americans rallied to support their president, giving him an 82 percent approval rating. Kennedy was amazed by the development: "My God, it's as bad as Eisenhower. The worse I do, the more popular I get.")

Then in 1961 East Germany built a wall to keep East Berliners from escaping to West Berlin. The wall became a stark reminder of the vulnerability of the democratic enclave of West Berlin. In an emotional speech at the wall, Kennedy excited West Berliners when he declared:

All free men, wherever they may live, are citizens of Berlin, and, therefore, as a free man, I take pride in the words *"Ich bin ein Berliner."*

A year later, when Kennedy learned that the Soviet Union was sending nuclear missiles to Cuba—only ninety miles from Florida—he ordered the navy to blockade Cuba. Tensions were high, and many believed that the two great powers were on the verge of war. After about a week, however, the Soviet Union removed their missiles.

Most historians cite the Test Ban Treaty—an agreement among the United States, the Soviet Union, and Great Britain to end atmospheric testing of nuclear weapons—as Kennedy's major accomplishment. Upon signing the treaty, Kennedy noted:

Today the fear is a little less and the hope a little greater: For the first time we have been able to reach an agreement which can limit the dangers of this [nuclear] age.

Six weeks later Kennedy was assassinated as he rode next to his wife in a motorcade traveling through Dallas. The youngest man ever elected president, he was also, at forty-six, the youngest president to die in office.

☆　☆　☆

We stand today on the edge of a new frontier—the frontier of the 1960s—a frontier of unknown opportunities and perils—a frontier of unfulfilled hopes and threats. ☙

Let the word go forth from this time and place, to friend and foe alike, that the torch has been passed to a new generation of Americans—born in this century, tempered by war, disciplined by a hard and bitter peace, proud of our ancient heritage and unwilling to witness or permit the slow undoing of those human rights to which this nation has always been committed and to which we are committed today at home and around the world.

Let every nation know, whether it wishes us well or ill, that we shall pay any price, bear any burden, meet any hardship, support any friend, oppose any foe to assure the survival and the success of liberty. ☙

The New Frontier of which I speak is not a set of promises—it is a set of challenges. It sums up not what I intend to offer the American people, but what I intend to ask of them. ☙

And so, my fellow Americans: Ask not what your country can do for you—ask what you can do for your country. ♭

Sure it's a big job, but I don't know anyone who can do it better than I can.
(on the presidency)

Those who make peaceful revolution impossible make violent revolution inevitable.

My father always told me that all businessmen were sons of bitches, but I never believed it till now.
(on price increases by steel industry executives)

Every American ought to have the right to be treated as he would wish to be treated, as one would wish his children to be treated. This is not the case.

Our task now is not to fix the blame for the past, but to fix the course for the future.

Let us never negotiate out of fear, but let us never fear to negotiate.

I do not think it altogether inappropriate to introduce myself. I am the man who accompanied Jacqueline Kennedy to Paris, and I have enjoyed it.

If a free society cannot help the many who are poor, it cannot save the few who are rich. ‘

When we got into office, the thing that surprised me most was to find that things were just as bad as we'd been saying they were.

I don't think the intelligence reports are all that hot. Some days I get more out of *The New York Times*.

It's much easier to make speeches than it is to finally make the judgments, because unfortunately your advisers are frequently divided. If you take the wrong course, and on occasion I have, the President bears the burden, responsibility, quite rightly. The advisers may move on to new advice.

Congressmen are always advising Presidents to get rid of presidential advisers. That's one of the most constant threads that run through American history, and Presidents ordinarily do not pay attention.

The path we have chosen for the present is full of hazards, as all paths are, but it is one most consistent with our character and courage as a nation and our commitments around the world. The cost of freedom is always high, but Americans have always paid it. And one path we shall never choose, and that is the path of surrender or submission. ◄
(*announcing the blockade of Cuba*)

The world is very different now. For man holds in his mortal hands the power to abolish all forms of human poverty and all forms of human life. ●

Men no longer debate whether armaments are a symptom or cause of tensions. The mere existence of modern weapons—ten million times more destructive than anything the world has ever known, and only minutes away from any target on earth—is a source of horror, of discord, of distrust . . . The risks inherent in disarmament pale in comparison to the risks inherent in an unlimited arms race. ●

Franklin Roosevelt started his campaign here in Ohio. I don't know what has happened to politics, but whenever I read about the 1932 campaign, Franklin Roosevelt stayed in Albany all winter, spring, summer, didn't go to the convention until he was nominated. He then took a boating trip up the coast of Maine with his son, started his campaign late in September, made some speeches, and was elected by a tremendous majority.

I want every American to stand up for his rights, even if he has to sit down for them. •

No one has been barred on account of his race from fighting or dying for America—there are no "white" or "colored" signs on the foxholes or graveyards of battle.

Any dangerous spot is tenable if brave men will make it so.

Forgive your enemies, but never forget their names.

It was involuntary. They sank my boat.
(on being asked how he became a hero)

A child miseducated is a child lost.

When power leads man toward arrogance, poetry reminds him of his limitations. When power narrows the area of man's concern, poetry reminds him of the richness and diversity of his existence. When power corrupts, poetry cleanses.

What can you expect from that zoo?
(on Congress)

We, the people, are the boss, and we will get the kind of political leadership, be it good or bad, that we demand and deserve.

Domestic policy can only defeat us; foreign policy can kill us. ☀

Acting on our own, by ourselves, we cannot establish justice throughout the world; we cannot ensure its domestic tranquillity, or provide for its common defense, or promote its general welfare, or secure the blessings of liberty to ourselves and our posterity. But joined with other free nations, we can do all this and more. ☀

When at some future date the high court of history sits in judgment on each one of us—recording whether in our brief span of service we fulfilled our responsibilities to the state—our success or failure, in whatever office we may hold, will be measured by the answers to four questions—were we truly men of courage . . . were we truly men of judgment . . . were we truly men of integrity . . . were we truly men of dedication?

I think this is the most extraordinary collection of talent, of human knowledge, that has ever been gathered together at the White House, with the possible exception of when Thomas Jefferson dined alone.

(at a reception for Nobel Prize winners)

Victory has a thousand fathers but defeat is an orphan. ☀

Any system of government will work when everything is going well. It's the system that functions in the pinches that survives.

What we need now in this nation, more than atomic power, or air power, or financial, industrial, or even manpower, is brain power. The dinosaur was bigger and stronger than anyone else—but he was also dumber. And look what happened to him. ☀

Let us resolve to be masters, not the victims, of our history, controlling our own destiny without giving way to blind suspicions and emotions.

I have just received the following telegram from my generous Daddy. It says, "Dear Jack: Don't buy a single vote more than is necessary. I'll be damned if I'm going to pay for a landslide."

I believe that this nation should commit itself to achieving a goal, before this decade is out, of landing a man on the moon and returning him safely to the earth.

The great enemy of the truth is very often not the lie—deliberate, contrived, and dishonest—but the myth—persistent, persuasive, and unrealistic.

Finally, it should be clear by now that a nation can be no stronger abroad than she is at home. Only an America which practices what it preaches about equal rights and social justice will be respected by those whose choice affects our future.

There is inherited wealth in this country and also inherited poverty.

Washington is a city of southern efficiency and northern charm.

☆ LYNDON BAINES JOHNSON ☆

36th President

Birth: August 27, 1908   Death: January 22, 1973
Term: November 22, 1963–January 20, 1969

THE JOHNSON (LYNDON) PRESIDENCY

- *Vietnam War expands (1963–69)*

- *The Civil Rights Act becomes law (1964)*

- *Medicare and Medicaid created (1965)*

- *The Water Quality Act (1965), the Clean Water Restoration Act (1966), the Clean Air Act (1965), and the Air Quality Act (1967) passed*

- *Dr. Martin Luther King and Senator/presidential candidate Robert Kennedy assassinated (1968)*

Upon his birth outside of Johnson City, Texas, Johnson's father set his expectations a bit low when he told his neighbors that "a United States senator is born today."

Johnson grew up amid hardship in Texas, earning spare cash however he could, as a hired hand, a shoeshine boy, and an animal trapper. At his mother's urging and with her coaching, Johnson learned the alphabet by the age of two and to read by the age of four. Although bright, he disliked schoolwork, and was often cited for misbehavior throughout his elementary-school years. "LBJ" graduated from Johnson City High School as president of his class (no other member of the graduating class of six wanted the job), and a few days later he ran away with friends to California. Soon broke, he secured a series of odd jobs, including picking fruit and washing clothes, before he returned home to Texas and entered Southwest Texas State Teachers College. Upon graduation he landed a job teaching public speaking and debate at a high school in Houston.

In 1931 he worked for Richard M. Kleberg's campaign for Congress. When Kleberg won, Johnson joined him in Washington and moved into the Dodge Hotel, where many congressional secretaries resided. In his first night at the hotel, determined to learn as much as he could as quickly as possible, Johnson took four showers in the communal bathroom and the next morning brushed his teeth five times at ten-minute intervals. He was on his way, dazzling Capitol Hill with his energy and abilities.

Among those he impressed were Sam Rayburn and Franklin Roosevelt, who soon appointed Johnson as Texas director of the National Youth Administration. This provided him with the political base to make a successful run for Congress in 1937. After a failed run for the U.S. Senate in 1941, he succeeded in 1948, winning by only 87 votes out of 900,000 cast, thus earning the nickname "Landslide Lyndon." This election was the first of his many in which vote fixing was charged. Even Johnson liked to joke about a small Mexican-American boy found crying in the streets of a Texas town. A neighbor asked the boy what was the matter, and the child complained that his father hadn't come to see him. "Why, son," the neighbor declared, "you know your daddy's been dead these last six years!" "I know," said the boy, "but he came back last Tuesday to vote for Lyndon Johnson, and he didn't even stop to see me."

In 1934 Johnson met journalism student Claudia Alta Taylor, better known as "Lady Bird." Although she declined his marriage proposal on their first date, his persistence resulted in a wedding only two months later (Johnson purchased a ring from Sears, Roebuck for $2.50). After four miscarriages, Lady Bird eventually gave birth to two daughters, Lynda Bird and Luci Baines (thus the entire family—including the dog, Little Beagle Johnson, had the initials L.B.J.).

In 1960 Johnson set his eyes on the presidency, only to lose the Democratic nomination to John F. Kennedy. He settled for the vice presidency. Then on November 22, 1963, at 2:30 P.M., an hour and a half after President Kennedy was pronounced dead, cut down by an assassin, Johnson took the oath of office for the presidency in the cabin of *Air Force One* at Love Field in Dallas. Over the next nine months, Johnson managed to win congressional approval for all the key elements in Kennedy's legislative program. In November 1964, he won the presidential election over Barry Goldwater with 61.1 percent of the popular vote, topping FDR's record of 60.8 percent in 1936.

No other American president was as skillful as Johnson at handling Congress—none of his thirty vetoes was overridden. The bills championed by Johnson guaranteed voting rights to southern blacks; ended racial discrimination in public accommodations; provided federal aid to education for the first time; created the Medicare system, the Model Cities Program, the Office of Economic Opportunity, and the job corps; and set aside millions of acres of new parkland wilderness.

But these many accomplishments were overshadowed by his Vietnam policy. When he took over the presidency, there were only 25,000 noncombat troops in Vietnam, and total American combat deaths numbered 109. By the time he left office, over 30,000 Americans had died in Vietnam. The war and his health eventually forced Johnson to withdraw from the 1968 presidential election.

He retired to the 360-acre LBJ Ranch in Texas where he wrote his memoirs, gave several major media interviews, and tended to the day-to-day operations of the ranch. He died on January 22, 1973, and was buried in the tiny family cemetery about 100 yards from his birthplace.

☆ ☆ ☆

All I have I would have given gladly not to be here today.
(*address following John F. Kennedy's burial*)

An assassin's bullet has thrust upon me the awesome burden of the Presidency. I am here to say that I need the help of all Americans, in all America.

What in the name of conscience will it take to pass a truly effective gun-control law? Now in this new hour of tragedy, let us spell out our grief in constructive action.

I'd rather have him inside the tent pissing out, than outside pissing in.
(*on keeping J. Edgar Hoover as FBI director*)

Never trust a man whose eyes are too close to his nose.

This is what America is all about. It is the uncrossed desert and the unclimbed ridge. It is the star that is not reached and the harvest that is sleeping in the unplowed ground.

A president's hardest task is not to do what is right but to know what is right.

I never trust a man unless I've got his pecker in my pocket.

The promise of America is a simple promise: Every person shall share in the blessings of this land. And they shall share on the basis of their merits as a person. They shall not be judged by their color or by their beliefs, or by their religion, or by where they were born, or the neighborhood in which they live.

If we quit Vietnam, tomorrow we'll be fighting in Hawaii, and next week we'll have to fight in San Francisco.

If you've got 'em by the balls, their heart and mind will follow.

I just knew in my heart that it was not right for Dick Nixon to ever be President of this country.

If we become two people—the suburban affluent and the urban poor, each filled with mistrust and fear of the other—then we shall effectively cripple each generation to come.

Just like the Alamo, somebody damn well needed to go to their aid. Well, by God, I'm going to Vietnam's aid.

The central lesson of our time is that the appetite of aggression is never satisfied. To withdraw from one battlefield means only to prepare for another.

The women of America represent a reservoir of talent that is still underused. It is too often underpaid, and almost always underpromoted.

You know, Congress can't take much at once. If you take a jigger of bourbon at a time, you can drink for a long time. But if you drink a pint all at once, it'll come up on you.

We are a nation of lovers and not a nation of haters. We are a land of good homes, decent wages and decent medical care for the aged. Yes, we want a land of hope and happiness but never a land of harshness and hate.

Of course, I may go into a strange bedroom every now and then that I don't want you to write about, but otherwise you can write everything.
(*to the press*)

Our own freedom and growth have never been the final goal of the American dream. We were never meant to be an oasis of liberty and abundance in a worldwide desert of disappointed dreams. Our nation was created to help strike away the chains of ignorance and misery and tyranny wherever they keep man less than God wants him to be.

We must change to master change.

Evil acts of the past are never rectified by evil acts of the present.
(*on civil disobedience*)

There is no American right to loot stores, or to burn buildings, or to fire rifles from the rooftops. That is crime—and crime must be dealt with forcefully and swiftly, and certainly—under the law.

We must throw open the doors of opportunity. But we also must equip our people to walk through those doors.

We have talked long enough in this country about equal rights. We have talked for one hundred years or more. It is time now to write it in the books of law.

Freedom is not enough. You do not wipe away the scars of centuries by saying: Now you are free to go where you want, and do as you desire, and choose the leaders you please. You do not take a person who for years has been hobbled by chains and liberate him, bring him to the starting line of a race and then say, "you are free to compete with all the others," and still justly believe that you have been completely fair. Thus it is not enough just to open the gates of opportunity. All citizens must have the ability to walk through those gates. This is the next and most profound stage of the battle for civil rights. We seek not just legal equity but human stability, not just equality as a right and a theory but equality as a fact and equality as a result.

I do not want to be the President who built empires or sought grandeur or extended dominion. I want to be the President who helped the poor find their own way and who protected the right of every citizen to vote in every election.

We are not about to send American boys nine or ten thousand miles away from home to do what Asian boys ought to be doing for themselves.
(*October 21, 1964*)

He [Senator Barry Goldwater] wants to repeal the present and veto the future.

The test before us as a people is not whether our commitments match our will and our courage; but whether we have the will and the courage to match our commitments.

The Great Society is a place where every child can find knowledge to enrich his mind and to enlarge his talents. . . . It is a place where the city of man serves not only the needs of the body and the demands of commerce but the desire for beauty and the hunger for community. . . . It is a place where men are more concerned with the quality of their goals than the quantity of their goods.

So here is the Great Society. It's the time—and it's going to be soon—when nobody in this country is poor. . . . It's the time—

and there's no point in waiting—when every boy or girl has the right to all the education that he can absorb. It's the time when every slum is gone from every city in America, and America is beautiful. It's the time when man gains full dominion under God over his destiny. It's the time of peace on earth and goodwill among men.

If you have a mother-in-law with only one eye and she has it in the center of her forehead, you don't keep her in the living room. *(on his hesitation to discuss America's military progress in Vietnam)*

I'd rather give my life than be afraid to give it. *(on his decision to walk in Kennedy's funeral procession)*

To conclude that women are unfitted to the task of our historic society seems to me the equivalent of closing male eyes to female facts.

The presidency has made every man who occupied it, no matter how small, bigger than he was; and no matter how big, not big enough for its demands.

It is the common failing of totalitarian regimes that they cannot really understand the nature of our democracy. They mistake dissent for disloyalty. They mistake restlessness for a rejection of policy. They mistake a few committees for a country. They misjudge individual speeches for public policy.

I report to you that our country is challenged at home and abroad: that it is our will that is being tried and not our strength; our sense of purpose and not our ability to achieve a better America.

I'm tired. I'm tired of feeling rejected by the American people. I'm tired of waking up in the middle of the night worrying about the war.

Being president is like being a jackass in a hailstorm. There's nothing to do but stand there and take it.

If you let a bully come in your front yard, he'll be on your porch the next day and the day after that he'll rape your wife in your own bed.

I don't believe I'll ever get credit for anything I do in foreign affairs, no matter how successful it is, because I didn't go to Harvard.

I knew from the start if I left a woman I really loved—the Great Society—in order to fight that bitch of a war . . . then I would lose everything at home. My hopes . . . my dreams.

Once we considered education a public expense; we know now that it is a public investment.

When I get out of that car, you can just see them light up and feel the warmth coming up at you . . . Those Negroes go off the ground. They cling to my hands like I was Jesus Christ walking in their midst.

I just don't understand those young people. Don't they realize I'm really one of them? I always hated cops when I was a kid, and just like them I dropped out of school and took off for California. I'm not some conformist middle-class personality.

He's like a Spanish horse, who runs fa|y debating contest and later
nine lengths and then turns around an|al level. Said his debating
he'll do something wrong in the end.|f slide around an argument
(on Richard Nixon) |he could take any side of a
|high-school class, second in
Five dollars invested in population c|served as president of the
dollars invested in economic growth. |rm that promised, "A Dance
|nt of his graduating class at
Free speech, free press, free religion|s admitted to the California
yes, the right of petition . . . well, the|ed law in Whittier (he was
|iice company, which failed
Democracy is a constant tension betw|e navy (1942–46).
in the arsenal of truth, there is no gr|even, married Thelma Cath-
|l years earlier, when Pat had
A long time ago down in Texas I lear|l high school and act in the
to hell and making him go there are t|of this pretty new teacher.
|posite her. That very same
A town that can't support one lawyer |he was nuts or something,"
|Lady, Mrs. Nixon promoted
I believe in the tight fist and the o|pided publicity.
money and an open mind to the need|turned to California and was
|). He then served as a U.S.
I seldom think of politics more than |ent (1953–61). He narrowly
|John F. Kennedy, lost the
The Great Society leads us along thre|and then returned to the
and liberation. |ity.
|k. He launched a smooth-
Voting is the first duty of democracy.|y and won in a close race
|rey (President Johnson had
War is always the same. It is young m|n as president is considered
their promise. It is trying to kill a ma|hdrew United States troops
well enough to hate. Therefore, to kn|the Soviet Union. In 1972,
is still madness in this world. |licy, he was reelected by a
|IcGovern. But trouble was

brewing. Police arrested five men who had burglarized the head-
quarters of the Democratic National Committee in Washington,
D.C., at the Watergate building complex. Some of those men
worked, or had worked, for various committees operating out of
Nixon's White House. An intensive investigation eventually discovered that nearly all Nixon's appointees at the White House, and
the president, were blatantly sidestepping the Constitution in an
effort to cover up the administration's criminal activity. Nixon se-
cretly recorded conversations evincing this conspiracy in his own
office. Once those tapes were released to the public, voters at last
heard the man his enemies had claimed Nixon was—a foul-
mouthed, conniving liar. Historian Fawn Brodie says of Nixon's
compulsive lying, "Nixon lied to gain love, to shore up his gran-
diose fantasies, to bolster his ever-wavering sense of identity. He
lied in attack, hoping to win . . . and always he lied, and this most
aggressively, to deny that he lied."

Those Nixon officials convicted of or pleading guilty to unlawful
activity were White House counsel John Dean, presidential appointments secretary Dwight Chapin, special presidential counsel
Charles Colson, chief domestic affairs adviser John D. Ehrlichman,
presidential chief of staff H. R. Haldeman, White House consultant E. Howard Hunt, personal attorney to the president Herbert
Kalmbach, White House aide Frederick Larue, White House assistant Gordon Liddy, White House aide Jeb Stuart Magruder, attorney general John Mitchell, White House aide Herbert Porter,
and commerce secretary Maurice Stans.

Facing impeachment proceedings, Nixon became the first president to resign his office.

Nixon retired to San Clemente, California, then later to New
York City and Saddle River, New Jersey. In 1974, he accepted
from his successor, President Gerald Ford, a "full, free, and absolute pardon" for all federal crimes that he "committed or may
have committed or taken part in" while president. Throughout his

retirement he wrote books, traveled throughout the world, and on occasion was consulted by his successors in the White House.

In 1994, on April 22, he died in New York City from complications of a stroke.

☆ ☆ ☆

Let us begin by committing ourselves to the truth—to see it like it is, and tell it like it is—to find the truth, to speak the truth, and to live the truth.
(on accepting the GOP presidential nomination in 1968)

You don't win campaigns with a diet of dishwater and milk toast.

We have no sense of arrogance—we honestly, almost naively, like people and want to get along with them. We lack often a sense of subtlety but that will come after a few hundred more years of civilization.
(on Americans)

The word *politics* causes some people lots of trouble. Let us be very clear—*politics* is not a dirty word.

There is one thing solid and fundamental in politics: the law of change. What's up today is down tomorrow.

One vote is worth a hundred obscene slogans.

I would have made a good pope.

What are our schools for if not indoctrination against communism?

There is nothing more wearing than to suppress the natural impulse to meet a crisis head-on, using every possible resource to achieve victory.

I'm an introvert in an extrovert profession.

The American leader class has really had it in terms of their ability to lead. It's really sickening to have to receive them at the White House as I often do and to hear them whine and whimper, and that's one of the reasons why I enjoy very much more receiving labor leaders and people from middle America who still have character and guts and a bit of patriotism.

Once you're in the stream of history you can't get out.

Your mind must always go, even while you're shaking hands and going through all the maneuvers. I developed the ability long ago to do one thing while thinking about another.

I never felt the "there but for the grace of God go I" reaction to Kennedy's death that many people seemed to imagine I would. After eight years as vice president I had become fatalistic about the danger of assassination.

You cannot win a battle in any arena merely by defending yourself.

I am going to campaign up and down America until we drive the crooks and the Communists and those that defend them out of Washington.

It is time for the great silent majority of Americans to stand up and be counted.

We were faced by an organization that had equal dedication and unlimited money that was led by the most ruthless group of political operators ever mobilized for a presidential campaign.
(on the Kennedy campaign team of 1960)

The people's right to change what does not work is one of the greatest principles of our system of government.

If there is anything I want to do before I die, it is to go to China. If I don't, I want my children to.

One reason we found the Chinese appeared to be so agreeable to deal with was their total lack of conceit or arrogance.

We've got to stop using the classrooms and the kids as the cutting edges of social and economic problems that will have to be solved elsewhere. Our goal should be education, not litigation.

Always remember others may hate you but those who hate you don't win unless you hate them. And then you destroy yourself.

Neutrality where the Communists are concerned means three things: we get out; they stay in; they take over.

As I looked at America's position in the world and examined our relations with other nations, I could see that the central factor in 1968 on the eve of my presidency was the same as it had been in 1947 . . . America now, as then, was the main defender of the free world against the encroachment and aggression of the Communist world.

Communist leaders believe in Lenin's precept: Probe with bayonets. If you encounter mush, proceed; if you encounter steel, withdraw.

If being a liberal means federalizing everything, then I'm no liberal. If being a conservative means turning back the clock, denying problems that exist, then I'm no conservative.

The ability to be cool, confident, and decisive in crisis is not an inherited characteristic but is the direct result of how well the individual has prepared himself for battle.

Going through the necessary soul-searching of deciding whether to fight a battle, or to run away from it, is far more difficult than the battle itself.

The finest steel has to go through the hottest fire.

Success is not a harbor but a voyage with its own perils to the spirit. The game of life is to come up a winner, to be a success, or to achieve what we set out to do. Yet there is always the danger of failing as a human being. The lesson that most of us on this voyage never learn, but can never quite forget, is that to win is sometimes to lose.

Voters quickly forget what a man says.

The favorite cliché of those who advocate summit talks regardless of the circumstances is, "Talking is always better than fighting." This, however, is not the only choice. Talking is not better than not talking when you do not know what you are going to talk about.

The kids, like all kids, loved the dog [Checkers], and I just want to say this, right now, that regardless of what they say about it, we are going to keep it.

When the President does it, that means that it is not illegal.

Politics is an art and a science. Politicians are, in the main, honorable, above average in their intellectual equipment, and effective in getting action on problems that less practical people only talk or write about. An individual has to be a politician before he can be a statesman.

You won't have Nixon to kick round anymore because, gentlemen, this is my last press conference.

I don't give a shit what happens. I want you all to stonewall it, let them plead the Fifth Amendment, cover up or anything else, if it'll save it—save the plan. That's the whole point.
(*from the Watergate tapes*)

This office is a sacred trust and I am determined to be worthy of that trust.

I made mistakes but in all my years of public life I have never profited, never profited from public service. I've earned every cent. And in all of my years in public life I have never obstructed justice. . . . I welcome this kind of examination because people have got to know whether or not their President is a crook. Well, I'm not a crook. I've earned everything I've got.

Our Presidents want publicity, but above all, they want results. We should applaud rather than condemn them when they resist the insatiable demands of the media in order to do the job they were elected to do.

I have never been a quitter. To leave office before my term is completed is abhorrent to every instinct in my body.
(*on his resignation from the presidency*)

We are faced with a choice between the work ethic that built this nation's character—and the new welfare ethic that could cause the American character to weaken.

My strong point, if I have a strong point, is performance. I always do more than I say. I always produce more than I promise.

Certainly in the next fifty years we shall see a woman president, perhaps sooner than you think. A woman can and should be able to do any political job that a man can do.

Under the doctrine of separation of powers, the manner in which the president personally exercises his assigned executive powers is not subject to questioning by another branch of government.

Government enterprise is the most inefficient and costly way of producing jobs.

I believe in building bridges, but we should build only our end of the bridge.

Our chief justices have probably had more profound and lasting influence on their times and on the direction of the nation than most presidents have had.

The media are far more powerful than the president in creating public awareness and shaping public opinion, for the simple reason that the media always have the last word.

I urged my audiences to be Lincoln Republicans: liberal in their concern for people and conservative in their respect for the rule of law.

☆ GERALD RUDOLPH FORD ☆

38th President

Birth: July 14, 1913
Term: August 9, 1974–January 20, 1977

THE FORD PRESIDENCY

- *Former President Nixon granted unconditional pardon (1974)*
- *United States Bicentennial (1976)*
- *Final Communist victory in Southeast Asia (1975–76)*

In 1939, Gerald Ford and his girlfriend, Phyllis Brown, were the featured personalities in a *Look* magazine article about a weekend in the life of the "beautiful people." The photos showed the couple modeling winter sports clothing at a ski resort in Vermont. This episode made Ford the first president to have been a model.

Ford was born to Leslie Lynch King and Dorothy Ayer Gardner. While he was still an infant, his mother—reportedly after frequent beatings by her husband—fled with her son to the safety of her parents' home in Grand Rapids, Michigan. In 1916, a year after her divorce, Dorothy married Gerald R. Ford, who adopted her son, and they renamed him accordingly.

Young Ford, an Eagle Scout, was a spirited, hardworking, and popular child who willingly did chores and enjoyed sports. His adoptive father owned and operated the Ford Paint and Varnish Company. The company managed, just barely, to stay afloat during the Depression and the family's circumstances were modest at best. Academically, Ford performed well throughout his school years. Athletically, he excelled. Upon graduation from the University of Michigan, both the Detroit Lions and the Green Bay Packers offered him contracts to play professional football. He turned down both to study law at Yale, where he earned money for tuition coaching football (among those he coached were future senators Robert Taft, Jr., and William Proxmire). He graduated in the top third of his class, along with such future notables as Supreme Court Justice Potter Stewart, Secretary of State Cyrus Vance, and Peace Corps Director R. Sargent Shriver. Ford was admitted to the Michigan bar in June 1941. He practiced law in Grand Rapids until the United States entered World War II, at which time he joined the navy. Assigned to the light aircraft carrier *Monterey*, he experienced some of the fiercest battles of the South Pacific war.

He returned from the war to Grand Rapids and joined a large law firm. Cheerful and easygoing, he made many friends. In 1948 he was asked to run for Congress as a Republican. He was elected easily and was reelected for the next twenty years.

In 1948, Ford, thirty-five, married Elizabeth "Betty" Anne Bloomer, a recent divorcée of thirty. Nearly thirty years later she would be an extremely popular and respected First Lady, speaking out in support of women's rights, the Equal Rights Amendment, and liberalized abortion laws. After she underwent a radical mastectomy the First Lady's candor in discussing publicly what for many women had been a private tragedy helped to focus national attention on breast cancer and the importance of early detection. She also won praise for speaking freely of her struggle against addiction to alcohol and pain-killing drugs.

Throughout his many years in Congress, Ford's ambition was to become Speaker of the House. But the Speaker represented the majority party, and the Republicans continued to be the minority party. In 1973 Ford told his wife that it seemed unlikely he would ever become Speaker and he had therefore decided to run for Congress once more, in 1974, then retire in 1976.

But in 1973, when Spiro T. Agnew was accused of taking bribes and resigned from the vice presidency in disgrace, Ford was President Nixon's choice for vice president. When Nixon resigned in

August 1974, Ford became the first man to be president without ever having run for the office of president or vice president.

Ford became president of a country very divided over the issues of Vietnam (Had the war been conducted correctly? What had it accomplished? Was the withdrawal of American troops an admission of defeat?) and Richard Nixon (Should he be tried? Or should Watergate be allowed to become history as soon as possible?). One month after taking office, Ford granted a full pardon to Nixon.

During his presidency, Ford signed the Campaign Reform Law (1974); kept New York City out of default with $2.3 billion in federal loans (1975); offered a clemency program for Vietnam-era draft evaders and deserters (1974); extended the benefits of the 1965 Voting Rights Act to Spanish-speaking and other language minorities (1975); and signed the Helsinki Agreement, which eased East-West tensions by pledging noninterference in each other's internal affairs (1975).

Although he had never had any driving ambition to be president, Ford found that he enjoyed the job. He decided to seek election for a full term as president. But the economy was awful—inflation was out of control and unemployment was rising—and some voters refused to forgive Ford for his pardon of Nixon. Ford lost a very close election to Democrat Jimmy Carter.

Ford retired to Rancho Mirage, California. He has written his memoirs, maintains an active speaking schedule, golfs, skis, and serves on the boards of numerous corporations.

☆ ☆ ☆

I'm a Ford, not a Lincoln.

I am acutely aware that you have not elected me as your president by your ballots, so I ask you to confirm me with your prayers.

If we want to restore confidence in ourselves as working politicians, the first thing we all have to do is to learn to say No.

It can go on and on, or someone must write "The End" to it. I have concluded that only I can do that. And if I can, I must.
(on Watergate, announcing his pardon of Richard Nixon)

A government big enough to give you everything you want is a government big enough to take from you everything you have.

Truth is the glue that holds governments together. Compromise is the oil that makes governments go.

It's the quality of the ordinary, the straight, the square, that accounts for the great stability and success of our nation. It's a quality to be proud of.

You can literally move mountains, mine the oceans, master the energy of the sun, and climb the highest peak of all—world peace. It won't be easy. But the achievements of the Tinley Park Titans weren't won easily either.
(speech to Tinley Park High School, Illinois)

When I became President, I did not want to have a powerful chief of staff. Wilson had his Colonel House, Eisenhower his Sherman Adams, Nixon his Haldeman, and I was aware of the trouble those top assistants had caused my predecessors.

The American people want a dialogue between them and their President . . . And if we can't have that opportunity of talking with one another, seeing one another, shaking hands with one another, something has gone wrong in our society.
(following two assassination attempts)

It's discouraging how hard it is for a President to slice any large chunks from a $305 billion budget.

One of the enduring traits of the nation's capital is that bureaucrats *survive*.

Teddy Roosevelt . . . once said, "Speak softly and carry a big stick." Jimmy Carter wants to speak loudly and carry a fly swatter.

The White House staff [under Richard Nixon] viewed Congress in much the same way that the chairman of the board of a huge corporation regards his regional sales managers.

The Constitution is the bedrock of all our freedoms; guard and cherish it; keep honor and order in your own house; and the republic will endure.

You don't need a lot of bureaucrats looking over your shoulder and telling you how to run your life or how to run your business. We are a people who declared our independence two hundred years ago, and we are not about to lose it now to paper shufflers and computers.

When I talk about energy, I am talking about jobs. Our American economy runs on energy. No energy—no jobs.

I have come to the conclusion that the public interest is no longer served by repetition of my previously expressed belief that on the basis of all the evidence known to me and to the American people, the President [Richard Nixon] is not guilty of an impeachable offense.

I guess it just proves that in America anyone can be President.

He was one of the few political leaders I have ever met whose public speeches revealed more than his private conversations. *(on Ronald Reagan)*

I believe that truth is the glue that holds Government together, not only our Government, but civilization itself.

☆ JAMES EARL CARTER ☆

39th President

Birth: October 1, 1924
Term: January 20, 1977–January 20, 1981

THE CARTER PRESIDENCY

- *Camp David Accords (1978)*

- *Canal Zone ceded to Republic of Panama (1979)*

- *United States officially recognizes the People's Republic of China (1979)*

- *United States Embassy personnel taken hostage in Iran (1979)*

"Jimmy" Carter was such a national unknown when he decided to run for president that people made a joke of it, asking "Jimmy who?" Just two years before being elected president, Carter appeared on television's "What's My Line?" and nearly stumped the panel. Even his own mother, when told of his plans to run for president, asked, "President of what?"

Carter was born in Wise Hospital in Plains, Georgia (the first president born in a hospital). When he was four, his family moved from Plains to nearby Archery, a largely black community, where Jimmy spent the remainder of his childhood. Although the Carters were well-off by community standards, they had neither electricity nor running water.

Well behaved, hardworking, and eager, Carter was the model student. In 1946, he graduated from the United States Naval Academy, fifty-ninth in a class of 820. His intention was to become a career naval officer, with the further aspiration to be chief of naval operations.

On July 7, 1946, Ensign Jimmy Carter, twenty-one, married (Eleanor) Rosalynn Smith, eighteen. She eventually served as bookkeeper for the Carter peanut business and helped build it into a prosperous enterprise. When she was First Lady, the president valued her advice; and like Eleanor Roosevelt before her, Mrs. Carter pushed herself to overcome her basic shyness so that she might deliver speeches to bolster her husband's many political and policy efforts.

Carter served in the navy from 1946 to 1953. In 1951 he joined the nuclear submarine program, studying nuclear physics at Union College. He was personally chosen by Admiral Hyman Rickover to serve as engineering officer aboard the *Sea Wolf*, one of the world's first atomic submarines.

In 1953, Carter returned to Plains to take over the family farm and peanut brokerage business upon the death of his father. He steadily improved production levels and expanded the business, which by 1979 had made him a millionaire. He became active in local civic affairs, emerging as a voice of reason during the desegregation crises of the 1950s and 1960s. He served in the Georgia State Senate (1963–67) and as governor of Georgia (1971–75).

In 1976, Carter shocked the country by capturing the Democratic party nomination for president with primary victories in New Hampshire and Iowa. He was a national unknown running on a platform promoting unification among all peoples and restoring trust in government. He then bested President Ford in the general election, becoming the first president elected from the Deep South since Zachary Taylor in 1848.

As president, Carter quickly put his moderate-to-left agenda into action, pardoning Vietnam War draft evaders on his first day in office. He strengthened laws protecting the environment, eased the eligibility for food stamps, put human rights at the cornerstone of his administration's foreign policy, and pushed to turn over control of the Panama Canal to Panama. On the foreign-affairs front, his crowning achievement was the Camp David Accords. These agreements resulted from thirteen days of intense, highly personal negotiations, in which three heads of state (Carter, Anwar Sadat of Egypt, and Menachem Begin of Israel) hammered out two documents—a framework for peace in the Middle East and a framework for the conclusion of a peace treaty between Egypt and Israel.

Domestically, Carter shouldered the blame for the nation's poor economy. When the oil-producing countries of the Middle East raised oil prices, the price of almost everything else rose as well. Interest rates were so high that few people could borrow money to build new homes, and few businesses could borrow to expand or buy new equipment. The solution was hardly clear; and those legislative initiatives that Carter did request were seldom passed by Congress.

Without a doubt, the low point of Carter's presidency and the key reason he failed to be reelected was the seizure of fifty-two Americans, who were held hostage by Iran in the American Embassy in Tehran. Americans were shocked and angry as negotiations for the release of the hostages dragged on for more than a year. Carter's popularity nosedived. The hostages were eventually released on Inauguration Day, 1981, as the new president, Ronald Reagan, was taking office.

Upon his retirement to Plains, Carter worked to revive the family peanut business, which had gone into deep debt while in a blind trust during his presidency. He has authored books, lectures frequently, and has undertaken diplomatic missions on behalf of his successor presidents, notably in North Korea and Haiti during the

Clinton administration. He is an activist in the areas of housing and human rights.

☆ ☆ ☆

We are, of course, a nation of immigrants, but some of us too often forget that the question isn't when we came here, but why we came here. Our nation has been called a melting pot. I think of it more as a mosaic, one to which many groups make their own distinct contributions.

Watch me closely during the campaign because I won't be any better a president than I am a candidate.

No poor, rural, weak, or black person should ever again have to bear the additional burden of being deprived of the opportunity for an education, a job, or simple justice.
(*inaugural address as governor of Georgia, 1971*)

The passage of the civil rights acts during the 1960s was the greatest thing to happen to the South in my lifetime.

Our American values are not luxuries but necessities—not the salt in our bread but the bread itself. Our common vision of a free and just society is our greatest source of cohesion at home and strength abroad—greater than the bounty of our material blessings.

We were sure that ours was a nation of the ballot, not the bullet, until the murders of John Kennedy, Robert Kennedy, and Martin Luther King, Jr.

It has now been thirty-five years since the first atomic bomb fell on Hiroshima. The great majority of the world's people cannot remember a time when the nuclear shadow did not hang over the earth. Our minds have adjusted to it, as after a time our eyes adjust to the dark.

The . . . purchase of unnecessary military equipment is undoubtedly the most wasteful element in American government.

A strong nation, like a strong person, can afford to be gentle, firm, thoughtful, and restrained. It can afford to extend a helping hand to others. It's a weak nation, like a weak person, that must behave with bluster and boasting and rashness and other signs of insecurity.

Whatever starts in California unfortunately has an inclination to spread.

We must adjust to changing times and still hold to unchanging principles.

If the misery of others leaves you indifferent and with no feeling of sorrow, then you cannot be called a human being.

. . . if I'm elected, at the end of four years or eight years I hope people will say, "You know, Jimmy Carter made a lot of mistakes, but he never told me a lie."

As President I will not be able to provide everything that every one of you might like. I am sure to make many mistakes. But I can promise you that you will never have the feeling that our needs are being ignored, or that we have forgotten who put us in office.

A simple and a proper function of government is just to make it easy for us to do good and difficult for us to do wrong.

You have given me a great responsibility: to stay close to you, to be worthy of you and to exemplify what you are.

I personally think that he did violate the law, that he committed impeachable offenses. But I don't think that he thinks he did. (*on Richard Nixon*)

The experience of democracy is like the experience of life itself—always changing, infinite in its variety, sometimes turbulent and all the more valuable for having been tested by adversity.

If you fear making anyone mad, then you ultimately probe for the lowest common denominator of human achievement.

The number of votes available to the sponsors of a tax bill [are] almost exactly proportional to the number of loopholes added to the legislation.

Human rights is the soul of our foreign policy, because human rights is the very soul of our sense of nationhood.

I don't know, it may be that poor people are the only ones who commit crimes but I do know that they are the only ones who serve prison sentences.

I've looked on a lot of women with lust. I've committed adultery in my heart many times. This is something that God recognizes I will do—and I have done it—and God forgives me for it. (*quote from* Playboy *magazine interview*)

If I ever give another interview on the biblical sin of pride and lust, it will be to the reporter from *Our Sunday Visitor*.

America did not invent human rights. In a very real sense . . . human rights invented America.

In a very Christian way, as far as I'm concerned, he can go to hell. *(on the Reverend Jerry Falwell)*

☆ RONALD WILSON REAGAN ☆

40th President

Birth: February 6, 1911
Term: January 20, 1981–January 20, 1989

THE REAGAN PRESIDENCY

- *Sandra Day O'Connor becomes first woman justice of the United States Supreme Court (1981)*

- *President wounded in assassination attempt (1981)*

- *United States troops invade Granada and oust Cuban forces (1983)*

- *Iran-Contra scandal (1985–89)*

The only professional actor to become president, Ronald Reagan is thus the only president to have costarred with a chimpanzee (1951's *Bedtime for Bonzo*). When in 1966 Jack Warner learned that Reagan was running for public office, he immediately replied, "No, no, no, no. You've got it all wrong. *Jimmy Stewart* for governor, Ronald Reagan for best friend."

Ronald Wilson Reagan was born in a rental apartment above a bakery in Tampico, Illinois. His father, on seeing his bawling child for the first time, said, "For such a little bit of a fat Dutchman, he makes a hell of a lot of noise." The nickname "Dutch" stuck. Reagan's family lived in various Illinois communities until he was nine, when they settled permanently in Dixon. Reagan remembers his lower-middle-class childhood with fondness. He was an average-to-good student, but his studies competed with his extracurricular activities such as sports and school plays. He graduated from Eureka (Illinois) College in 1932 and for the next five years worked as a radio broadcaster, announcing baseball and football games throughout the Midwest.

He then moved to Hollywood and switched to acting for the next thirty years (1937–65), playing the lead in B pictures and supporting roles in A movies. His pictures included *Love Is on the Air*, *Sergeant Murphy*, *Brother Rat*, *Dark Victory*, *Hell's Kitchen*, *Knute Rockne—All American*, *Kings Row*, *That Hagen Girl*, *The Girl from Jones Beach*, *The Winning Team*, and *Bedtime for Bonzo*.

In the midst of his Hollywood career, from 1942 to 1945, Reagan served in the United States Army Air Force First Motion Picture Unit, where he narrated training films.

Reagan, twenty-eight, married actress Jane Wyman, twenty-six, in 1940 at the Wee Kirk o'Heather wedding chapel near Hollywood. The two eventually separated, reconciled briefly, and in May 1948 separated permanently. Reagan was the first president to have been divorced. At age forty-one, in 1952, Reagan married Nancy Davis, thirty. As First Lady, Mrs. Reagan was very active in the administration, advising the president on a variety of issues, including staffing. In a scandal that surfaced shortly after they left office, it was revealed that Mrs. Reagan had arranged the president's daily schedule on the advice of a San Francisco astrologer.

Reagan served as president of the Screen Actors Guild (1947–52 and 1959–60) and, politically, underwent a transformation from what he called "a near hopeless hemophiliac liberal" Democrat who "bled for causes" to a staunchly conservative Republican. In 1950 he campaigned against Richard Nixon in his bid for the U.S. Senate; in 1952 and 1956 he joined Democrats-for-Eisenhower; by 1960, he was delivering speeches (two hundred of them) for Richard Nixon, and in 1962 he changed his voter registration to Republican. In 1964 he delivered an extremely effective thirty-minute television address on behalf of Republican presidential nominee Barry Goldwater.

He ran for and won the governorship of California in 1967 and held that office until 1975. After unsuccessful bids for the Republican presidential nomination in both 1968 and 1976, he secured the nomination in 1980. Incumbent Carter was vulnerable because of the Iranian hostage crisis and a terrible economy, and Reagan won in a landslide. At age sixty-nine, he was the oldest man ever to be elected president. He would win again four years later over Walter Mondale, Carter's vice president, with the largest number of electoral votes in history.

Reagan focused much of his presidency on the economy and the cold war. His program of supply-side economics came to be called Reaganomics: he drastically reduced the taxes of the wealthy in a bid to stimulate spending and investment and simultaneously cut money in programs for the poor, the aged, the environment, and national parks. He vastly increased military spending, driving the federal budget deficit in 1984 up to more than $180 billion.

In 1987, Soviet leader Mikhail Gorbachev and President Reagan signed the Intermediate-Range Nuclear Forces (INF) Treaty in which both countries agreed to destroy hundreds of medium- and short-range missiles.

On March 30, 1981, Reagan was shot in an assassination attempt ("I forgot to duck," he joked). The bullet entered his left side, bounced off his seventh rib, punctured and collapsed a lung, and lodged an inch from his heart. Despite his age of seventy, he made a quick and complete recovery. Twelve days after the shooting, he returned to the White House.

Throughout his presidency, global terrorism increased, and although the Reagan administration took a strong public "no negotiation" position, the White House covertly negotiated with terrorists, selling them high-tech weaponry in exchange for concessions, and thus even abetting further terrorist acts. Toward the end of his presidency, much of the administration's momentum was stalled by the ongoing Iran-Contra scandals, which revealed the White House's complex system of selling arms to Iranian-backed terrorists and diverting the profits to illegally aid rebel forces, the "contras," in Nicaragua.

By the time Reagan left office, the cold war with the Soviet Union had nearly thawed, and several East Bloc nations had either broken free or were on the verge of breaking free from Soviet domination. The United States was also the biggest debtor nation in the world. Reagan's twin intentions to swing the balance of Soviet-American power and to change the course of domestic economics had been met, for better and for worse.

I've always believed that this land was set aside in an uncommon way, that a divine plan placed this great continent between the oceans to be found by a people from every corner of the earth who had a special love of faith, freedom and peace.

America is too great for small dreams.

The Chinese philosopher, Sun Tzu, 2,500 years ago said winning a hundred victories in a hundred battles is not the acme of skill; to subdue the enemy without fighting is the acme of skill. A truly successful army is one that, because of its strength and ability and dedication, will not be called upon to fight because no one will dare to provoke it.

Trees cause more pollution than automobiles.

If the Soviet Union will join with us in our effort to achieve major arms reduction we will have succeeded in stabilizing the nuclear balance. Nevertheless it will still be necessary to rely on the specter of retaliation—on mutual threat, and that is a sad commentary on the human condition.

It's time we reduced the federal budget and left the family budget alone.

Free enterprise is a rough and competitive game. It is a hell of a lot better than a government monopoly.

Millions of individuals making their own decisions in the marketplace will always allocate resources better than any centralized government planning process.

Somewhere along the way these folks in Washington have forgotten that the economy is business. Business creates new products and new services. Business creates jobs. Business creates prosperity for our communities and our nation as a whole.

Entrepreneurs share a faith in a bright future. They have a clear vision of where they are going and what they are doing, and they have a pressing need to succeed. If I didn't know better, I would be tempted to say that "entrepreneur" is another word for America.

The very key to our success has been our ability, foremost among nations, to preserve our lasting values by making change work for us rather than against us.

[One] of the simple, but overwhelming, facts of our time is this: of all the millions of refugees we have seen in the modern world, their flight is always away from, not toward, the communist world.

Excellence does not begin in Washington.

Our Constitution is to be celebrated not for being old, but for being young.

Why is the Constitution of the United States so exceptional? . . . Just three words: We the people. In . . . other constitutions, the Government tells the people of those countries what they are allowed to do. In our Constitution, we the people tell the Government what it can do.

You go to bed at night knowing that there are things you are not aware of.
(on the presidency)

The one thing our Founding Fathers could not foresee—they were farmers, professional men, businessmen giving of their time and effort to an idea that became a country—was a nation governed by professional politicians who had a vested interest in getting re-elected. They probably envisioned a fellow serving a couple of hitches and then eagerly looking forward to getting back to the farm.

We built it, we paid for it, it's ours, and we're going to keep it.
(on the Panama Canal)

Bureaucracy does not take kindly to being assailed and isn't above using a few low blows and a knee to the groin when it fights back. Knowing this I have become extremely cautious in dealing with government agencies.

A tree is a tree—how many more do you need to look at?

Government always finds a need for whatever money it gets.

We do not face large deficits because American families are undertaxed; we face those deficits because the federal government overspends.

The taxpayer—that's someone who works for the federal government but doesn't have to take a civil-service exam.

We are a nation that has a government—not the other way around. And that makes us special among the nations of the earth.

The most powerful force we can enlist against the federal deficit is an ever-expanding American economy, unfettered and free.

Regimes planted by bayonets do not take root.

Too often, the demands of prosperity and security are viewed as competitors when, in fact, they are complementary, natural and necessary allies.

In the past two decades, we have created hundreds of new programs to provide personal assistance. Many of these programs may have come from a good heart, but not all have come from a clear head.

If I could paraphrase a well-known statement by Will Rogers that he never met a man he didn't like—I'm afraid we have some people around here who never met a tax they didn't like.

History teaches that wars begin when governments believe the price of aggression is cheap.

GEORGE HERBERT

☆ WALKER BUSH ☆

41st President

Birth: June 12, 1924
Term: January 20, 1989–January 20, 1993

THE BUSH PRESIDENCY

- *Invasion of Panama (1989)*
- *Collapse of Communism*
- *Persian Gulf War (1990–91)*

Bush's mother, Dorothy Walker Bush (1901–92), who was an excellent and versatile athlete (she smacked a home run in a family softball game just minutes before going to the hospital to deliver her first child), offered five dollars to the first of her four sons to beat her in tennis. George collected the prize at age sixteen.

Bush was born in the family's home in Milton, Massachusetts. (In June! Bush was the first president to have been born in June, so that after forty-one presidents, a president has now been born in all twelve months.) When he was an infant, his family moved to Greenwich, Connecticut, where he lived a very comfortable childhood, his needs being tended to by a nanny, a housekeeper, and the family handyman-chauffeur, who drove young Bush to school and out on his early dates. He especially enjoyed his maternal grandfather's home in Kennebunkport, Maine, where he learned to boat and fish.

His teachers at Phillips Academy recall Bush as an unremarkable student who did little more than what was expected of him. Outside of the classroom, however, he was busy, as president of his senior class, captain of the baseball and soccer teams, and an editor on the school newspaper.

Immediately after graduation from prep school, on his eighteenth birthday, Bush joined the navy. He was, for a time, the war's youngest U.S. Navy pilot. Serving in the Pacific, Bush flew more than fifty combat missions. On September 2, 1944, his plane was shot down. The only crew member to survive, Bush just barely escaped being captured when he was rescued by an American submarine.

Navy Lieutenant Bush, twenty, married Barbara Pierce, nineteen, on January 6, 1945 after having met at a Christmas dance. Both claimed it was "love at first sight" (he was the first boy she ever kissed). Her mixed feelings about Bush's decision to give up the familiar security of the privileged East Coast and strike out on his own were severely tested when one of their first homes in Texas was a cramped apartment with a common bathroom that they shared with a mother-daughter team of prostitutes. A popular First Lady who was active in promoting adult literacy, Barbara Bush was considered direct, spirited, independent, and refreshingly unpretentious.

After the war, Bush entered Yale, where he majored in economics and played on the college baseball team. After graduation, he successfully entered the booming oil business in Texas. Beginning in 1952—and in great part because his father was now serving as a senator from Connecticut—Bush became active in the Republican party, campaigning for Eisenhower and serving as chairman of the Harris County (Houston area) Republican party. In 1966 he was elected to the U.S. House of Representatives and served there until 1971. In 1969 Bush visited Lyndon Johnson to seek his advice on whether he should give up a safe House seat or run for the

Senate. Bush entered the senatorial race after Johnson provided this assessment: "The difference between being a member of the Senate and a member of the House is the difference between chicken *salad* and chicken *shit*." Bush resigned from the House and lost the Senate campaign but was soon appointed by President Nixon as ambassador to the United Nations (1971–73). He then served as chairman of the Republican National Committee (1973–74), chief liaison in China (1974–75), and director of the Central Intelligence Agency. He made a bid for the Republican nomination for president in 1980 but lost out to Ronald Reagan, who then chose Bush as his running mate.

After Reagan's retirement, Bush secured the Republican nomination for the 1988 race and easily defeated his Democratic opponent, Massachusetts Governor Michael Dukakis.

Bush's presidency was dominated by foreign affairs. During his administration, Soviet President Mikhail Gorbachev announced that the Soviet Union would no longer try to control the affairs of Eastern Europe. One by one, the Communist governments of Eastern Europe were toppled from within. In 1988, the Berlin Wall, the very symbol of the Iron Curtain, fell, and East and West Germany were reunited. In 1990, when Iraq invaded Kuwait, Bush convinced a group of nations, including Britain, France, Saudi Arabia, and Egypt, to combine armies and sweep Iraq's armies back out of Kuwait. The swift victory made Bush extremely popular.

But just as quickly, the economic boom of the Reagan years ended. In handling foreign affairs, Bush had clear goals and stuck to them. On the domestic side, what few bold ideas he had were often defeated by the Democrat-led Congress. Campaigning for reelection in 1992, Bush faced not only a fresh, young Democratic opponent, Bill Clinton, but also Ross Perot, a wealthy Texan who entered the race as an independent and who focused most of his ire on Bush, criticizing his economic and industrial policies.

After presiding over the end of the cold war and an overwhelming victory in the Gulf War, Bush was turned out of office after a single term.

☆ ☆ ☆

Appeasement does not work. As was the case in the 1930s, we see in Saddam Hussein an aggressive dictator threatening his neighbors.

America is never wholly herself unless she is engaged in high moral principle. We as a people have such a purpose today. It is to make kinder the face of the nation and gentler the face of the world.

The federal government too often treats government programs as if they are of Washington, by Washington and for Washington. Once established, federal programs seem to become immortal.

A campaign is a disagreement, and disagreements divide. But an election is a decision, and decisions clear the way for harmony and peace. I mean to be president of all the people, and I want to work for the hopes and interests not only of my supporters but of the governor's [Dukakis] and of those who didn't vote at all.

Surely a tired woman on her way to work at six in the morning on a subway deserves the right to get there safely. And surely, it's true that everyone who changes his or her life because of crime—from those afraid to go out at night to those afraid to walk in the parks they pay for—surely these people have been denied a basic civil right.

For more than forty years, America and its allies held communism in check and insured that democracy would continue to exist. And today, with communism crumbling, our aim must be to insure democracy's advance, to take the lead in forging peace and freedom's best hope, a great and growing commonwealth of free nations.

We're enjoying sluggish times and not enjoying them very much.

I have opinions of my own—strong opinions—but I don't always agree with them.

I'm not what you call your basic intellectual.

There's no difference between me and the president on taxes. No more nit-picking, Zip-a-dee-do-da. Now it's off to the races.
(Vice President George Bush regarding his working relationship with President Reagan)

Caribou like the pipeline. They lean up against it, have a lot of babies, scratch on it. There's more damn caribou than you can shake a stick at.
(dismissing environmentalists' concerns about the Alaskan pipeline's impact)

The notion of political correctness has ignited controversy across the land. And although the movement arises from the laudable desire to sweep away the debris of racism and sexism and hatred it replaces old prejudices with new ones. It declares certain topics off-limits, certain expressions off-limits, even certain gestures off-limits. What began as a crusade for civility has soured into a cause of conflict and even censorship.

If anyone tells you that America's best days are behind her, they're looking the wrong way.

A government that remembers that the people are its master is a good and needed thing.

Communism held history captive for years, and it suspended ancient disputes and it suppressed ethnic rivalries, nationalistic aspirations and old prejudices. As it has dissolved, suspended hatreds have sprung to life. . . . this revival of history ushers in a new era teeming with opportunities and perils . . .

To write off the United Nations' achievements in keeping the peace because of its inability to be effective in Czechoslovakia or Vietnam would be like writing off medical science because it has not yet found a cure for cancer.

This is a fact: Strength in the pursuit of peace is no vice; isolation in the pursuit of security is no virtue.

I see something happening in our towns and in our neighborhoods. Sharp lawyers are running wild. Doctors are afraid to practice medicine. And some moms and pops won't even coach Little League any more. We must sue each other less—and care for each other more.

Flag burning is wrong. I believe the importance of this issue compels me to call for a constitutional amendment.

The Congress will push me to raise taxes, and I'll say no, and they'll push, and I'll say no, and they'll push again and I'll say to them, read my lips, no new taxes.

This is America . . . a brilliant diversity spread like stars. Like a thousand points of light in a broad and peaceful sky.
(accepting the Republican nomination for the presidency)

WILLIAM JEFFERSON

☆ CLINTON ☆

42nd President

Birth: August 19, 1946
Term: January 20, 1993—

THE CLINTON PRESIDENCY

- *NAFTA: The North American Free Trade Agreement (1993)*
- *Brady Handgun Act (1993)*
- *Terrorists bomb New York City's World Trade Center (1993) and Oklahoma City federal building (1995)*
- *War in the former Yugoslavia*

William Jefferson Clinton has always loved politics. He ran for so many class and club offices that his high-school principal had to bar him from campaigning for any more.

Clinton is the first postwar, baby-boom-generation president. He was born in Hope, Arkansas, in 1946, to Virginia Cassidy. Clinton's father, William Jefferson Blythe, died in a freak car accident during the pregnancy. In 1950, Clinton's mother married Roger Clinton, an alcoholic who physically abused his wife, stepson, and son. Nonetheless, Bill legally changed his name to that of his stepfather, who died in 1967.

Clinton was a Boy Scout, sang in the church choir, listened to rock and roll, and formed a jazz combo with two friends in which they performed wearing sunglasses and were known as the Three Blind Mice. In 1956, he sat glued to the Democratic and Republican conventions, which nominated Governor Adlai Stevenson and President Dwight Eisenhower. In 1963, he was moved to tears by Martin Luther King's "I Have a Dream" speech. In the same year he traveled to Washington in the American Legion program Boys' Nation where, at a White House reception for the group, Clinton shook hands with President John F. Kennedy. That encounter had a profound effect on Clinton, and eventually the nation—he had decided on a career in politics.

An excellent student, Clinton won his school's Academically Talented Student Award, was a member of the National Honor Society, and made it to the semifinals of the National Merit Scholarship competition. He also won first place in a state saxophone contest.

Clinton graduated from Georgetown University and went on to Oxford in England as a Rhodes scholar. He next attended Yale University law school, where he assisted in the campaign of an antiwar candidate for senator from Connecticut. He also managed George McGovern's Texas campaign during his unsuccessful run for the presidency in 1972.

In 1975, Clinton, twenty-nine, married Hillary Rodham, twenty-seven, the first career woman and first lawyer to become First Lady. As First Lady, she broke precedent by occupying an office in the West Wing of the White House where the president's senior staff members work. Extremely active in the administration, she headed the President's Task Force on National Health Reform.

Upon graduation from law school in 1973, Clinton became a law professor at the University of Arkansas. He served as attorney general of Arkansas (1977–79), and twice as governor of Arkansas (1979–81 and 1983–92). The timing of his decision to run for the presidency was excellent. Because of President Bush's immense popularity after the Gulf War, many more obvious potential Democratic candidates declined to run for election, assuming that Bush had the race locked up.

In a campaign heavily affected by third-party candidate Ross

Perot, the presidential hopefuls spurned the standard news interview programs like *Meet the Press* in favor of informal talk shows hosted by entertainers like Phil Donahue, Arsenio Hall, and Larry King. In the end, Clinton and his vice presidential running mate and fellow baby boomer, Tennessee Senator Albert Gore (born in 1948), captured a generation of new voters and won back many of the Democrats who twelve years earlier had switched to Reagan.

Clinton has made two appointments to the Supreme Court—Ruth Bader Ginsberg and Stephen Breyer—and attempted to overhaul the nation's health care system.

With a Democratic Congress in place, the first two years of the Clinton presidency were very active. Legislation involving the economy, education, crime, health care, and trade were passed. The most notable of these in 1993 were the ratification of the North American Free Trade Agreement (NAFTA), the Brady Bill (which requires a five-day waiting period during which all potential handgun purchasers are submitted to a background check), the Family and Medical Leave Act, student-aid reform, and the National and Community Service Trust Act (AmeriCorps).

However, after mid-administration elections in 1994, the Republican party gained control of Congress and for the reminder of his term limited Clinton's ability to set and act upon national policy.

☆ ☆ ☆

My greatest fear is that student government . . . is going to be rejected unless it takes the lead in trying to stop the kind of failure exemplified by the following instances, all of which might not have been failures except for a lack of leadership initiative, or purposeful power and a grim determination:

1. We ought to have pushed harder for a five-game football schedule. We could have gotten it.

2. We ought to throw out, or at least boycott, the cafeteria's meal ticket system for men, which requires a deposit by parents on which Georgetown draws the interest . . .
(writing in the November 1966 issue of the Georgetown Courier, *a student publication of Georgetown University in Washington)*

My doctor ordered me to shut up, which will make every American happy.
(prompted by laryngitis)

Today, the average CEO at a major American corporation is paid one hundred times more than the average worker. Our government rewards that excess with a tax break for executive pay, no matter how high it is, no matter what performance it reflects. And then the government hands out tax deductions to corporations that shut down their plants here and ship our jobs overseas. That has to change.

I believe I'm a better authority than anybody else in America on my wife. I have never known a person with a stronger sense of right and wrong in my life—ever.

That's got every fire hydrant in America worried.
(on Dan Quayle's intention to be a "pit bull" in helping the Republicans retain the White House)

Isn't that like calling Moe the most intelligent of the Three Stooges?
(on being introduced as the smartest of the candidates seeking the Democratic presidential nomination)

When I was in England I experimented with marijuana a time or two, and I didn't like it, and I didn't inhale, and I never tried it again.

For too long we've been told about "us" and "them." Each and every election we see a new slate of arguments and ads telling us that "they" are the problem, not "us." But there can be no "them" in America. There's only us.

Though our challenges are fearsome, so are our strengths. And Americans have ever been a restless, questing, hopeful people. We must bring to our task today the vision and will of those who came before it.

There is nothing wrong in America that can't be fixed with what is right in America.

It is time to break the bad habit of expecting something for nothing, from our government or from each other. Let us all take more responsibility, not only for ourselves and our families but for our communities and our country.

Each generation of Americans must define what it means to be an American.

I refuse to be part of a generation that celebrates the death of communism abroad with the loss of the American dream at home.

For too long the young of the Middle East have been caught in a web of hatred not of their own making. For too long they have been taught from the chronicles of war; now we can give them the chance to know the season of peace.
(on the PLO/Israel peace negotiations)

Now it is our turn to strike a blow for freedom in this country. The freedom of Americans to live without fear that their own nation's health-care system won't be there for them when they need it.

I don't know whether it's the finest public housing in America or the crown jewel of prison life. It's a very isolating life.
(*on living in the White House*)

I miss the sort of heart and soul and fabric of life that was a part of every day when I got up and went to work in a state capital.

I am often troubled as I try hard here to create a new sense of common purpose . . . we oftentimes get so caught up in the battle of the moment, the heat of the moment . . . that sometimes we forget that we are all in this because we are seeking a good that helps all Americans.

I did not run for this job just to warm the seat. I desperately want to make a difference.

I like the job . . . The bad days are part of it. I didn't run to have a pleasant time, I ran to have the chance to change the country, and if the bad days come with it—that's part of life, and it's humbling and educational. It keeps you in your place.

America does not need a religious war. It needs reaffirmation of the values that for most of us are rooted in our religious faith.

Our objectives are clear. Our forces are strong, and our cause is right.
(*on sending American troops to the Persian Gulf*)

It was a real sort of southern deal. I had AstroTurf in the back. You don't want to know why, but I did.
(reminiscing about an El Camino pickup truck he once owned)

A new season of American renewal has begun . . . we must be bold.
(inauguration, January 1993)

I know it is unpopular. I know the timing is unpopular. I know the whole thing is unpopular. But I believe it is the right thing.
(on invading Haiti)

They may walk with a little less spring in their step, and the ranks are growing thinner, but let us never forget, when they were young, these men saved the world.
(in Normandy, on the fiftieth anniversary of the Allied landings there on June 6, 1944)

I don't suppose there's any public figure that's ever been subject to any more violent personal attacks than I have.

This was not a vote about the right of the president to choose a surgeon general. This was really a vote about every American woman's right to choose [whether or not to terminate her pregnancy].
(on congressional defeat of his surgeon general nominee)

☆ INDEX ☆

References to the text of the biographies include page number only. References to quotations include page number and quotation number. The first full quotation on a page is quotation 1.